A Turner's G
to Veneer Inlays

Ron Hampton

4880 Lower Valley Road, Atglen, PA 19310 USA

Dedication

To Barbara, Jennifer Beth, and Sarah: the three most important people in my life. Thank you! You can never know how much your love and support mean to me.

— Ron

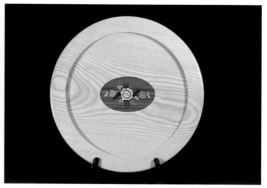

Contents

Introduction 3
Safety 4
Requirements of Turning Shapes for the Veneer 6
Inlays and Tools Needed 8
Practice Cuts 10
A Round Box with a Rose Inlay 13
Oval Inlay into a Platter 26
Banding a Beautiful Bowl Rim 34
Mixing Glass and Wood: Adding a Wood Base
   & Rim to a Glass Vase 46
Inlaying a Flat Oval Veneer into a Round Vase 58
Gallery 64

Copyright © 2003 by Ron Hampton
Library of Congress Control Number: 2002113979

Designed by Mark David Bowyer
Type set in Americana XBd BT/Humanist 521 BT

ISBN: 0-7643-1611-7
Printed in China

Published by Schiffer Publishing Ltd.
4880 Lower Valley Road
Atglen, PA 19310
Phone: (610) 593-1777; Fax: (610) 593-2002
E-mail: Schifferbk@aol.com
Please visit our web site catalog at **www.schifferbooks.com**
We are always looking for people to write books on new and related subjects. If you have an idea for a book please contact us at the above address.

This book may be purchased from the publisher.
Include $3.95 for shipping.
Please try your bookstore first.
You may write for a free catalog.

In Europe, Schiffer books are distributed by
Bushwood Books
6 Marksbury Ave.
Kew Gardens
Surrey TW9 4JF England
Phone: 44 (0)20-8392-8585
Fax: 44 (0)20-8392-9876
E-mail: Bushwd@aol.com
Free postage in the UK. Europe: air mail at cost

Introduction

Woodturners are artists who see the beauty that lies in wood. As turners, we are always looking for new and better ways to create art. We are always looking new and different ways to allow the beauty of wood to show through our art.

That is why I decided to write this book on how to inlay veneers into turned art. There are an infinite number of veneer inlay possibilities for the wood artist. The techniques are simple, but the results are beautiful. Inlaying veneer does require some patience, careful technique, and a few simple tools. But the results of these efforts will be beautiful pieces of art.

Adding veneer inlays to your turnings will make them more beautiful and will make them stand out from other turnings. This can give you a tremendous advantage at craft fairs and galleries.

Woodturning is experiencing tremendous growth in popularity around the world. Many people are finding that they now have the time and money to be able to enjoy new hobbies. Others find that they would like to slowly move into a new career direction. Woodturning is the perfect answer for many people. It is a wonderfully satisfying hobby and can be a terrific source of additional income. For the hobbyist, woodturning can be richly rewarding as a means of artistic expression and as a means of relaxation. For the professional, woodturning can be a pleasant lifestyle that gives the turner a desirable form of employment. Inlaying veneer into turned art allows you to carry your art to a higher level.

We will cover five beautiful veneer inlay projects that will get you well on your way to mastering inlaying veneer into turned art. Have fun and continue to learn. There is a whole world of possibilities in turning, and a lifetime of challenges!

Safety

Working with wood can be a lot of fun, and it can be very safe if you follow the safety rules and pay attention. However, any and all tools can be dangerous! So to have fun, and be safe at the same time it is necessary to follow some basic safety rules. It is also important to understand why we have the rules.

Veneer Safety

It is simple and easy to cut the rebates for veneer inlays when the job is properly done. However, there are a couple of safety precautions. There are three main areas where accidents could occur in the rebate cutting process.

1. First the rebate area is outlined with an Exacto™ knife or sharp utility knife. You must always be careful when working with a sharp knife to make sure that it does not get away from you. Be sure to use controlled motions and keep your fingers out of the way.

Figure 1. You must always be careful when working with a sharp knife to make sure that it does not get away from you. Be sure to use controlled motions and keep your fingers out of the way.

2. The bulk of the rebate material will be removed with a miniature router. You must be very careful to control the router and not let it get away from you.

Figure 2. The bulk of the rebate material will be removed with a miniature router. You must be very careful to control the router and not let it get away from you.

3. The final shaping of the rebate is done with a sharp chisel. It is very important that you do not drive the chisel into your hand. This should not be a problem since you will be making very small and delicate cuts.

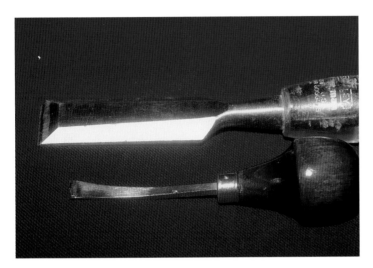

Figure 3. The final shaping of the rebate is done with a sharp chisel. It is very important that you do not drive the chisel into your hand. This should not be a problem since you will be making very small and delicate cuts.

Below are some additional safety tips on the safe use of the lathe.

Lathe Safety

1. Speed kills! That is true about drugs and cars ... and about machinery. You are turning an object with a lathe. If the object gets away from you or comes apart, it can become a lethal flying object

2. Sober and alert! When working in the shop you must always be sober and alert. If you are too tired or in too big of a hurry to do something the correct way, then it is time for you to quit and go to the house. You cannot do good work if you are compromised. In addition, it is very easy to get hurt.

3. Safety equipment: Always wear the proper safety equipment. This means that you always put a face shield on before turning on the lathe. **Always!!!** (See Figure 4.) Anytime you are making any dust, you must have a respirator or air filter on. (See Figure 5.) If you are too tired to wear the filter and face shield, then you are too tired to work. That is okay. Quit and go to the house. The more comfortable your safety equipment is, the more likely you are to use it. So shop around and get the best, most comfortable safety equipment you can find. (Notice I did not say the cheapest equipment you can find.) Safety equipment and procedures include, but are not limited to, the following:

1. A sturdy face shield;

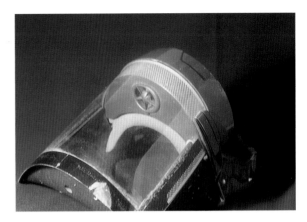

Figure 4. Anytime you are using power equipment, you must have a respirator and a sturdy face shield on.

2. Air filter or respirator;

Figure 5. Sears makes a good respirator with replaceable filters.

3. Shop apron with no loose sleeves or strings to get caught;
4. Plastic safety glasses;
5. No loose jewelry (watches, chains, rings), hair, or clothing;
6. **Nothing in the Line of Fire:** With your tool rest in place between you and the turning, any flying object will almost always travel in a straight line away from the lathe or straight up. Make sure that your friends or dog are not in the line of fire. Before I moved to my metal shop, I killed windows in my garage on two different occasions. (I know much more about speed control now. I also know how to fix windows.)
7. **No unattended machines:** If you leave the machine, turn it off. Never walk away from a running lathe. And never walk across the path of a running lathe. Do not let a friend watch in the line of fire.
8. **No vibrations:** Make sure that your turning is in balance and not causing the lathe to vibrate. Whenever possible, hold the turning at both ends by using your tailstock.

Requirements of Turning Shapes for the Veneer

Veneers can be inlaid into far more shapes than most people realize. Most turners think that a veneer can only be inlaid into the top of a box. Actually that is a nice application, which we will cover in detail. But there are many more applications for veneer inlays.

There are four different applications that we will cover in this book.

1. Inlaying a veneer into the lid of a box.

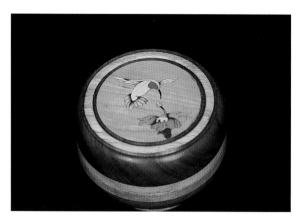

Figure 6. Inlaying a veneer into the lid of a box is a fun and easy project.

2. Inlaying a veneer into the bottom of a bowl or platter.

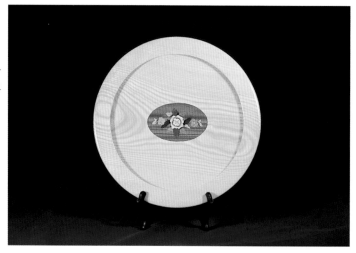

Figure 7. Inlaying a veneer into the bottom of a bowl or platter can make your platters really stand out.

3. Inlaying a strip veneer around the top of a bowl.

Figure 8. Inlaying a strip veneer around the top of a bowl will make your vase far more attractive.

4. Inlaying a circular or oval veneer into a tall round vase.

Figure 10. Edge banding a rim is a fun project that makes your rims far more attractive.

Figure 9. Inlaying a circular or oval veneer into a tall round vase is a challenging project but well worth the effort.

Requirements of Form

The form or shape of the turning is very important for the veneer inlay. Veneer inlays need a flat surface to lie into. This means that you must be very careful when designing the turned form. The area where the veneer is to be inlaid must be big enough and flat enough to accept the veneer.

In designing your form, it is best to have the veneer inlay before you actually start the project. It can be very frustrating to complete a turning and start to do your inlay, only to find out that the inlay does not fit the project.

The first project here is inlaying a veneer into the top of a box lid. The diameter of the box must be wide enough to accept the inlay. Also, the top of the box must be flat. This eliminates some artistic opportunities, but opens others.

To inlay a veneer in the bottom of a bowl, it is necessary to have a flat bottom that is large enough to accept the inlay. In addition, you must have access to the bottom of the bowl to be able to cut the rebate for the veneer. This means that it will be very difficult to make a veneer inlay at the bottom of a tall narrow vase.

Placing a veneer strip around the rim of the bowl is fairly simple design-wise. You just need to have a flat area wide enough for the veneer strip to lay in. (See Figure 10.)

Likewise, placing a veneer strip around the top of a bowl requires that you leave enough room to fit the size veneer that you choose. A lot of times you want a small bead on either side of the inlay. This requires that you leave additional room.

Placing a veneer in a platter is one of the simplest layout exercises. Usually you will place a round inlay inside a round platter. You might choose to cut this rebate while the platter is still on the lathe. If you are placing an oval inlay into an oval platter, you need to be sure of your placement before you start making a cut. (See Figure 11.)

If you want to place veneer inlay into freeform turned art, you will need to do some planning before you make the art form. A few minutes planning at the beginning of a project might save you hours of frustration later when you start trying to make a flat, stiff veneer fit into a curved surface.

Figure 11. Careful measurements are necessary in the placement of the veneers.

Inlays & Tools Needed

Unlike most new procedures in wood working, veneer inlays will require a minimum amount of new equipment. You will need to purchase some inlay veneers and you may need to purchase a mini-router. Everything else you already have!

Beautiful wood veneers are available from many woodworking supply stores. (See Figure 12.) Circular and oval veneers might be harder to find. I purchased mine from Woodworkers' Supply™ (1-800-645-9292). Circular and oval inlays will cost from $10.00 to $30.00 a piece. Inlay banding will cost about $4.00 per foot for a 1/16 inch wide veneer to about $10.00 per foot for 1/2-inch wide. (See Figure 13.) Prices will vary greatly depending on the designs and the quantities of exotic woods used.

Figure 14. A miniature router might be the most expensive item that you need to buy. I like the Sears laminate trimmer.

Figure 12. Beautiful wood veneers are available from many woodworking supply stores.

Figure 15. Your router needs to be able to make a smooth, flat cut.

Most of the other items you probably already have in your shop. (See Figures 16 and 17.) These include yellow glue and a sharp, thin blade knife. You will need to make a raid on the kitchen pantry to get some wax paper or aluminum foil. (See Figure 16.)

You will also need a supply of hose clamps. (See Figure 18.)

Figure 13. Veneer strips come in all sizes and designs.

A miniature router might be the most expensive item that you need to buy. It will cost about $110.00-130.00. My laminate trimmer/router came from Sears and I like it. (See Figures 14 and 15.) You will also need a 1/4- or 1/8-inch wide flat straight cutting bit for the router.

Figure 16. These items you probably already have: yellow glue, wax paper, and aluminum foil.

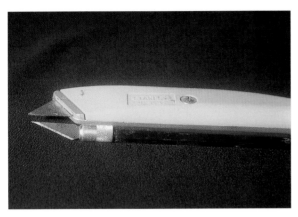

Figure 17. You will need a sharp utility knife or an Exacto™ knife.

Figure 18. An assortment of hose clamps are useful for veneer and segmented turning work.

Thickness Sanders

Thickness sanders are necessary pieces of equipment for the segmented turner. You can make a disc sander for your lathe that will work quite well. You can also purchase a $1,000 thickness sander if you plan on doing a lot of segmented turning. As a third alternative, you can purchase my machined steel thickness sander. (See Figure 19.) This consists of two 3/8-inch round steel plates with a Morse #2 taper machined on the end. This will sand the rings flat and parallel. In addition, the single Morse taper plate is used as a glue press for gluing up segments) I sell the single plate for $170 and both plates for $320. If you would like to order one, you can contact me at: **turngood@cableone.net, http:// www.woodturningplus.com**, or 903-794-5386.

Figure 19. My thickness sander consists of two 3/8-inch round steel plates with a Morse #2 taper machined on the end. This will sand the rings flat and parallel. (In addition, the single Morse taper plate is used as a glue press, for gluing up segments.) I sell the single plate for $170 and both plates for $320. If you would like to order one, you can contact me at **turngood@cableone.net, http:// www.woodturningplus.com**, or 903-794-5386.

Practice Cuts

Veneer inlay work requires a high degree of accuracy. There are many different types of veneers. (See Figure 20.) But they are all thin. The veneers are only 25/1000 of an inch thick. (See Figure 21.) This is the thickness of about twenty sheets of plain white paper. Once the veneer is glued in place you are able the finish sand the veneer only about 12/10,000 of an inch, which is about the thickness of ten sheets of paper. This is not a whole lot of thickness for error! So you need to have your rebate cut very accurately for depth.

Figure 20. There are many beautiful veneers for you to choose from.

Figure 21. The veneers are only 25/1000 of an inch thick.

In addition, it is very important to cut correctly for width. You, and everybody who sees your art, will closely inspect your glue line. They will say nothing about it if the glue line is perfect, but they will sure point out an open joint. If you have to make a mistake, it is best to have the rebate too small. If it is too small you just have some extra work to do in making the hole wider.

Extra Veneers Inlays

It is a good ideal to purchase a few extra inlays when you make your order. That way you can redo an inlay if you are not satisfied with your first try.

Practice Cuts

It is good to gain some practice making veneer rebates on scrap wood. You do not have to glue the veneer into the scrap wood; just make the correct rebate cuts. This will speed up your progress in mastering veneer inlays.

Veneer Strips

The easiest veneers to do are veneer strips that go around the outside of a round object. Start by turning a wood blank round. Lay a small piece of your veneer strip onto the turning. (See Figure 22.) Use a sharp pencil to mark on both sides of the veneer. Check to make sure that your line is correct. (See Figure 23.) Make a sharp straight in cut just on the inside of both lines. (See Figure 24.) This is best done with a sharp skew. Next clean out the wood in between the lines using a small round skew. (See Figure 25.) Test fit the veneer strip. (See Figure 26.) If the fit is too tight, use your skew to barely make the rebate wider.

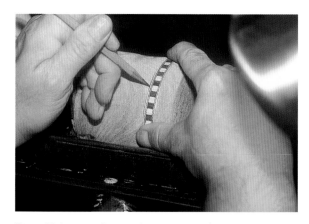

Figure 22. Lay a small piece of your veneer strip onto the turning. Use a sharp pencil to mark on both sides of the veneer.

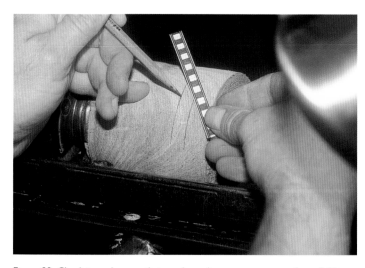

Figure 23. Check to make sure that you have drawn a correct set of parallel lines.

Figure 24. Make a sharp, straight in cut just on the inside of both lines. This is best done with a sharp skew.

Figure 27. To practice inlaying a round inlay, first flatten the top of a piece of scrap wood.

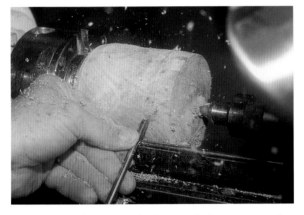

Figure 25. Clean out the wood in between the lines using a small round skew.

Figure 28. Use your calipers to measure the diameter of your round inlay. Transfer this measurement to your wood practice top.

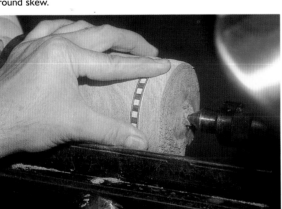

Figure 26. Test fit the veneer strip. If the fit is too tight, use your skew to barely widen the rebate.

Figure 29. Use a sharp skew and just barely cut inside the line.

Inlaying A Round Lid

Flatten the top of a piece of scrap wood. (See Figure 27.) Use your calipers to measure the diameter of your round inlay. Transfer this measurement to your wood practice top. (See Figure 28.) Use a sharp skew and just barely cut inside the line. Make a straight in cut a short distance. (See Figure 29.) Lay your skew flat to the tool rest and remove the center part of the rebate. (See Figure 30.) Clean out the entire circle to the same depth. Refine the butt joint carefully. (See Figure 31.) This should give you a very nice and clean joint. (See Figure 32.) Test fit the round inlay. It should fit perfectly. If not, start over by removing the small amount of wood adjacent to the rebate.

Figure 30. Make a straight in cut that is about 1/32 of an inch deep.

Figure 31. Lay your skew flat to the tool rest, and remove the center part of the rebate. .

Figure 32. Clean out the entire rebate to the same depth. Refine the butt joint carefully. This should give you a very nice and clean joint.

Oval Inlays

Practice making oval inlays cut on a soft wood like pine. Trace around the inlay using a sharp pencil. (See Figure 33.) You should get a smooth continuous line. (See Figure 34.) Use your sharp utility knife or Exacto knife to make a straight in cut all the way around. Be sure to brace your hands well so that you are cutting straight in and so that you cannot slip. (See Figure 35.) Use your router to route out the waste wood. Start from the center and work your way outward. (See Figure 36.) Work carefully and slowly bring your router close to the pencil line. Use good magnification so that you can see well. Also use good lighting. You can get a very accurate cut this way. Test fit the inlay into the rebate. You should have a very nice fit. (See Figure 37.)

Figure 33. Practice making oval inlays cut on a soft wood like pine. Trace around the inlay using a sharp pencil.

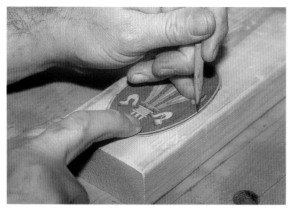

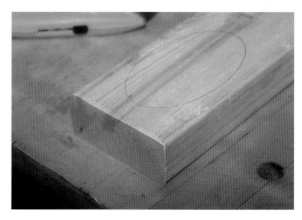

Figure 34. Your tracing should make a smooth, continuous line.

Figure 35. Use your sharp utility knife or Exacto™ knife to make a straight in cut just inside the pencil mark all the way around. Be sure to brace your hands well so that you are cutting straight in and cannot slip.

Figure 36. Use your router to remove the waste wood. Start from the center and work your way outward.

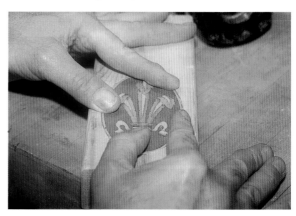

Figure 37. Work carefully and slowly with your router. Bring your router close to the pencil line. Use good magnification so that you can see well. Also use good lighting. You can get a very accurate cut this way. Test fit the inlay into the rebate. You should have a very nice fit.

A Round Box with a Rose Inlay

A nicely made round box is one of the most popular items that a turner can make. They make wonderful gifts and sell well at craft fairs. Boxes can be made quickly once you learn the techniques and can be made from small scraps of wood that are left over from other projects.

I was at a Texas Turn Or Two meeting one time when a member of the audience asked the demonstrator if he could turn a box in thirty minutes? He laughed and asked, "How many boxes do you want me to do in thirty minutes?" The man in the audience didn't know what to say. The demonstrator said, "OK, how about I make you a box in ten minutes." Most of us were dumb-founded. But yes he did make a nice box and finished it in about six minutes except for sanding.

We will not be trying to make a ten-minute box in this exercise, but it can be done. We will be learning how to make a nicely fitting box easily, and then we are going to do something special to it. We are going to inset a rose veneer inlay into our pretty box.

Getting Started

Gluing a Block

For veneer work, it is essential to control dimensional change in the turning as much as possible. Green, wet wood will move too much to make satisfactory inlays. For veneer work, you will always be starting with dry wood.

In this project, we will be using off cuts that are about 3 to 4 inches square. Do a test arrangement to make sure you like the visual impact of the color of the wood. (See Figure 38.) Here I wanted red Padauk for the top and bottom of the box. The middle is made from two layers of a white wood. I used oak in this case. With experience you could get by with only using one layer of white in the middle. But this is a learning experience and we want this to be easy.

Figure 38. Make a "dry" arrangement of your glue-up blocks. Make sure that you like the color arrangement.

The glue block will consist of two pieces of Padauk, two pieces of oak, and a piece of 3/4-inch plywood on each end. This makes a total of six pieces that we will glue together. Another pretty wood combination is to use black walnut for the outside layer and oak for the inside layer.

Gluing segments can be a mess. There are a few techniques that will help keep the glue under control. First use aluminum foil or wax paper on your work area. (See Figure 39.) This will help keep the glue from running all over the place. Second, try not to use too much glue.

Figure 39. Gluing segments can be a mess. Use aluminum foil or wax paper on your work area to keep the glue from running all over the place.

Start by laying the first 3/4-inch plywood block onto the center of the aluminum foil. Add a small dab of yellow glue on the center of the plywood. (See Figure 40.) Use a small stirring stick to spread the glue evenly over the entire square. I like to use small strips cut from leftover Formica.

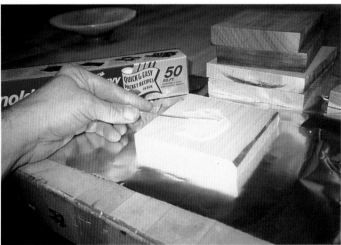
Figure 40. Apply a small dab of yellow glue on the center of the plywood. Use a small stirring stick to spread the glue evenly over the entire square.

Now place the first piece of Padauk onto the plywood. Press down and make circular motions. This will insure that you have a good glue joint. Ideally you would get just a bare trace of glue to express out all the way around the joint. (See Figure 41.) Do the same thing to the next piece of wood. Again make sure that the glue is evenly spread and that you have a good joint. Continue to do this until you have all six pieces glued together in a stack. (See Figure 42.)

Figure 41. You should get just a bare trace of glue to express out all the way around the joint when the pieces are pressed together.

Figure 42. Glue all of your squares of wood into a stack. Make sure that the glue is evenly spread and that you have good joints. Continue to do this until you have all six pieces glued together into a stack.

Squaring Up the Stack

Most likely your squares will not be all the same size. Lay the stack on its side and square up two sides of the stack. You will use these two square sides for finding the center of the stack eventually. (See Figure 42.)

Clamping to Dry

Now fold the aluminum foil around the glue stack. This will keep the excess glue in while it is clamped. (See Figure 43.) I use the vise on my worktable as a clamp. (See Figure 44.) You could just as easily use regular carpenter's clamps. Allow the yellow glue to dry overnight.

Remove the aluminum foil. Most of it will come off easily. Do not worry about the foil that sticks to the turning blank. It will turn off with no trouble. (See Figure 45.)

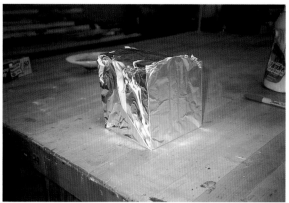

Figure 43. Squaring up the stack. Most likely your squares will not all be the same size. Lay the stack on its side, and square up two sides of the stack.

Figure 44. Clamp the glue up to dry. You can use regular clamps or a bench vise. Allow the yellow glue to dry overnight.

Figure 45. Remove the aluminum foil. Most of it will come off easily. Do not worry about the foil that sticks to the turning blank. It will turn off without difficulty.

Mounting to a Faceplate

Mark the center of the turning blank by using a straight edge, going corner to corner, or by using a center finder. (See Figure 46.) Make an indent in the center of the blank so that it will be easier to locate the faceplate. (See Figure 47.) If you have a center hole in your faceplate, put a screw in it and position the faceplate. If the center of the faceplate is open, then use a compass to draw a circle to help you center the faceplate.

Use eight 3/4-inch #8 metal screws to attach the faceplate to the turning blank. (See Figure 48.) Be sure that your screws stay in the plywood and do not enter the lid of the box. Place the faceplate and turning blank on the lathe. (See Figure 49.)

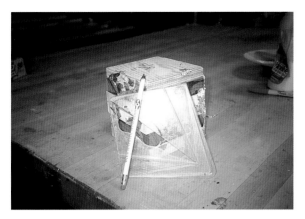

Figure 46. Mark the center of the turning blank by using a straight edge, going corner to corner, or by using a center finder.

Figure 47. Make an indent in the center of the blank so that it will be easier to locate the faceplate.

Figure 48. Use eight 3/4-inch #8 metal screws to attach the faceplate to the turning blank. Be sure that your screws stay in the plywood and do not enter the lid of the box.

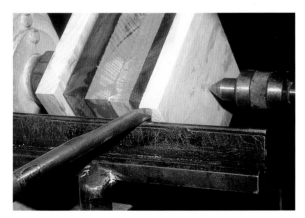

Figure 49. Place the faceplate and turning blank on the lathe. Adjust the tool rest so that your gouge is in line with the line drawn from the center of the headstock to the tailstock.

Turning the Box

Roughing Out

Screw the faceplate all the way onto the lathe. Bring the tailstock up and lock it into position. (See Figure 49.) Advance the live center into the plywood. Lock the live center into position. **Safety Note!! It is very important to always use a tailstock when possible.** The tailstock adds a tremendous amount of safety to your turning.

Adjust your tool rest so that your gouge is sitting on a line between the tailstock and the headstock. (See Figure 49.) This is always your starting position for a tool. You may decide to change this position, but this is a good starting point.

Set your lathe speed for a fairly slow speed, about 500 RPM. If you have variable speed, set it for about 250 RPM. Put your face shield on and stand to the side of the lathe, out of the line of fire. Turn the lathe on. If there is no vibration, you are ready to start turning. If there is vibration, you must do one of the following:

Reduce the speed of the lathe.
Rebalance the wood.
Use a different piece of wood.

Use your bowl gouge to rough out the blank. Point the gouge straight in and take very small bites. (See Figure 50.) This is not the time to get in a hurry. Slowly take small bits of wood, which will slowly round over the corners. As the turning blank becomes more round you will be able to take bigger bites with the gouge and to increase the speed of the lathe. (See Figure 51.)

Figure 50. Use your bowl gouge to rough out the blank. Point the gouge straight in, and take very small bites.

Figure 51. As the turning blank becomes more round, you will be able to take bigger bites with the gouge and will be able to increase the speed of the lathe.

You should never increase the speed of the lathe so much that it starts to vibrate. Use the side of your bowl gouge to make a shear cut. (See Figure 52.) Be sure that your bowl gouge is sharp.

Figure 52. **You should never increase the speed of the lathe so much that it starts to vibrate.** Use the side of your bowl gouge to make a shear cut.

This will allow you to make a smooth cylinder out of your turning blank.

A Joint Rebate

Cut a joint rebate in the middle of the turning blank. This will eventually divide the top from the bottom. Make the rebate with a 1/2-inch skew or a parting tool. The rebate should be 1/2-inch wide and about 1/2-inch deep. (See Figure 53.) Use a pencil to mark where you will part through the rebate. (See Figure 54.) Most of the rebate will be on the bottom of the box and will be used to make a nice fitting joint. A very small part of the rebate will be left on the topside of the rebate to allow you to quickly cut the correct size hole in the top of the box.

Figure 53. Cut a joint rebate in the middle of the turning blank.

Figure 54. Use a pencil to mark where you will part through the rebate.

Part through the rebate using a thin parting tool. I like the Chris Scott thin parting tool. (See Figure 55.) Be sure to have a very good hold on the thin parting tool as you make your cut. (See Figure 56.) If you have a weak hold on the tool, the friction of the turning can snap the tool out of your hand. This has happened to me on several occasions. I have smashed my finger a couple of times as a result. (I know this is difficult to picture, but you can smash your finger when you try to recover control and jerk the tool back down.)

Cut through the turning blank and put the top part of the box away for a while. (See Figure 56.)

Figure 55. Part through the rebate using a thin parting tool.

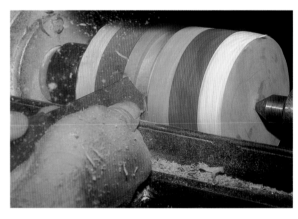

Figure 56. Be sure to have a very good hold on the thin parting tool as you make your cut. If you have a weak hold on the tool, the friction of the turning can snap the tool out of your hand.

Use your skew to widen the rebate on the bottom part of the box so that it is about 1/2-inch tall and 1/2-inch deep. (See Figure 57.) The rebate will not be this tall or deep on the finished box. But making the rebate this tall and deep will give you some room for error latter in the box-making process.

Figure 57. Use your skew to widen the rebate on the bottom part of the box so that it is about 1/2-inch tall and 1/2-inch deep.

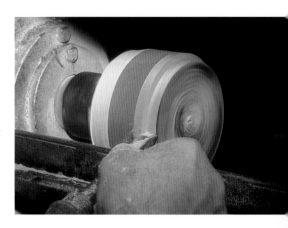

Rough Shaping the Box Exterior

Use your bowl gouge to rough shape the exterior bottom of the box. Round the bottom of the box. (See Figure 58.) Do not do final shaping at this time. Do not sand. If will be necessary to make adjustments when you put the lid onto the bottom.

Figure 58. Use your bowl gouge to rough shape the exterior bottom of the box. Round the bottom of the box. Do not do final shaping at this time.

Cut the Bottom Inside of the Box

It is now time to cut the inside of the bottom of the box. Use a pencil to mark the thickness of the final wall of the bottom. (See Figure 59.) Make a little dimple in the center of the box so that the drill bit has a starting place. (See Figure 60.) Place a piece of tape on your drill bit to mark how deep you want to drill. (See Figure 61.) Leave at least 1/2-inch for the thickness of your bottom. Your final bottom may be thinner than this, but you need to leave a little room for error. Cutting a hole through the bottom of your box can cause you to do some extra work. (And all turners have done this!!)

Figure 59. Cut the inside of the bottom of the box. Use a pencil to mark the thickness of the final wall of the bottom.

Figure 60. Make a little dimple in the center of the box so that the drill bit has a starting place.

Figure 61. Place a piece of tape on your drill bit to use as a depth gauge.

Put your drill bit into the dimple, and drill to the desired depth. (See Figure 62.) Remove your drill bit often to clear shavings. This will keep your drill bit from getting hot and lodged in the turning. If you do get your drill bit lodged in the turning you can remove it by letting it cool for a few minutes. You can usually unscrew the drill bit with some effort.

Figure 62. Drill out the center of the turning blank with your drill bit. This will make hollowing the center of the box much easier.

Use your parting tool to cut where the inside wall of the box will be. (See Figure 63.) Make this demarcation line a little thick for now. You can make this wall thinner after you have most of the box hollowed out. This demarcation cut helps you to control the cutting of the inside of the bowl. This step will not be necessary when you get comfortable using a bowl gouge.

Figure 63. Use your parting tool to cut where the inside wall of the box will be. Make this demarcation line a little thick for now. You can make this wall thinner after you have most of the box hollowed out. This demarcation cut will help you control the cutting of the inside of the bowl.

Use your bowl gouge to hollow the center of the bowl. Start from the center hole and cut toward the outside. (See Figure 64.) Remove about 1/8-inch of wood with each pass. Do not get too aggressive and cut too deep or too fast. Be careful as you reach your demarcation line. Cut very slowly here. Use your bowl gouge to make a continuous sweep from the center of the bowl to the edge of the rim. (See Figure 65.) (The funny pinky finger is from me taking the photograph as I make the cut. It gets a little tricky sometimes!!)

Figure 64. Use your bowl gouge to hollow the center of the bowl. Start from the center hole, and cut toward the outside.

Figure 65. Use your bowl gouge to make a continuous sweep from the center of the bowl to the edge of the rim.

Use a scraper to refine the inside of the box. Either one of these scrapers will do a fine job. (See Figure 66.) I also have several homemade scrapers that do an excellent job. A sharp scraper and a fine touch can create very fine shavings. Sand the inside of the box. I usually like to sand to about 400-grit on small boxes. (See Figure 67.) Apply finish to the inside of the box at this time. I like to use a mixture of Deft cellulose diluted 50/50 with lacquer thinner. Apply with a paper towel and let it stay wet for about twenty seconds before wiping off with the same paper towel. (See Figure 68.) Allow this to dry for a couple of minutes and then reapply as many times as you want to.

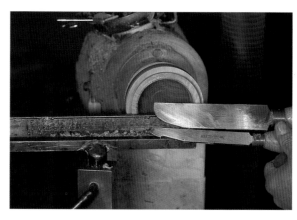

Figure 66. A sharp scraper and a fine touch can create very fine shavings. Sand the inside of the box.

Figure 67. Sand to about 400-grit on small boxes. Make sure that you have removed all irregularities.

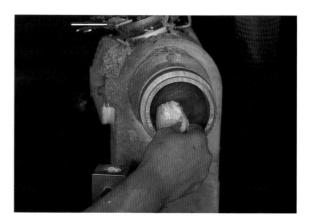

Figure 68. Apply finish to the inside of the box at this time.

Turning the Top

Next mount a faceplate to the piece that will be the top of the box. This is easy to do because you have an indent from the live center that marked the center of the turning. Use your pencil to highlight the rebate area. (See Figure 69.) You will remove the wood from the center of the box to this line. The correct fitting of the lid will be at this line. Use your bowl gouge to make a small depression or dimple in the bottom of the top. (See Figure 70.) This will allow your drill to seat in the center of the lid. (See Figure 71.) Drill out the center of the lid. Be careful to leave plenty of thickness in the top of the lid.

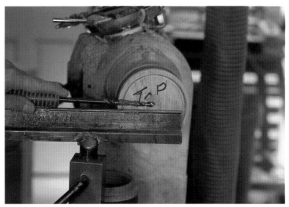

Figure 71. Drill out the center of the lid. Be careful to leave plenty of thickness in the top of the lid.

Use your bowl gouge to hollow the inside of the lid. (See Figure 72.) The top of the lid should be at least 1/2-inch thick at this point. Remember that you have to sand it smooth and then make a rebate in the top of the box for the inlay to seat into. Make long sweeps with your bowl gouge from the center of the lid to the outside. (See Figure 73.)

Figure 69. Use your pencil to highlight the rebate area of the lid. Leave the wall a little thick at this time.

Figure 72. Use your bowl gouge to hollow the inside of the lid. The top of the lid should be at least 1/2-inch thick at this point.

Figure 70. Remove the wood from the center of the box to the pencil line. The correct fitting of the lid will be at this line.

Figure 73. Make long sweeps with your bowl gouge from the center of the lid to the outside.

Use your scraper to smooth the inside of the lid. (See Figures 74 and 75.)

Figure 74. A sharp scraper does a good job on the inside of a box.

Figure 75. Use your scraper to smooth the inside of the lid.

Use your skew to remove the last little bit of the original rebate and make the edge of the lid flat. (See Figure 76.)

Figure 76. Use your skew to make the edge of the lid flat, and remove the last little bit of the original rebate.

Adjusting the Fit of the Lid

The bottom of the box should not fit into the lid at this point. It should be too tight by the thickness of one or two pencil lines. Use a straight scraper to cut the inside straight wall of the lid. (See Figure 77.) Cut a very small amount and then test the fit. (See Figure

78.) I normally will make about fifteen test fits before I have the fit that I want. The fit at this time should be snug. (See Figure 79.) You will make it loose later, after the inlay has been completed.

Figure 77. Use a straight scraper to cut the inside straight wall of the lid.

Figure 78. Make small cuts with the straight scraper to lighten the tightness of the lid.

Figure 79. The fit at this time should be snug. You will make it loose later, after the inlay has been completed.

You will notice in Figure 79 that I have used two faceplates in this exercise. You can do this if you have two faceplates, or you can use one faceplate. Two faceplates have the advantage of not having to realign the faceplate when you need to remount the turning.

Use your scraper to make the inside top of the lid smooth. (See Figure 80.) Sand the inside of the lid, being careful to not sand enough to loosen the fit of the lid. (See Figure 81.) Apply finish to the inside of the lid.

Figure 80. Use your scraper to make the inside top of the lid smooth.

Figure 81. Sand the inside of the lid, being careful not to sand enough to loosen the fit of the lid. Then apply finish to the inside of the lid.

Rough Shape the Outside of the Lid

Use your bowl gouge to round over the top of the lid. (See Figure 82.) Do not do final shaping and sanding at this time. Now use a thin parting tool to part off the lid from the faceplate. (See Figure 83.) Be sure to have a very good grip on the parting tool. (See Figure 84.) (I bet you are wondering how I took this photograph since you can see both of my hands.)

Figure 82. Use your bowl gouge to round over the top of the lid. Do not do final shaping and sanding at this time.

Figure 83. Use a thin parting tool to part off the lid from the faceplate.

Figure 84. Be sure to have a very good grip on the parting tool.

I ran out of plywood to mount on the top of my Padauk, so I used a piece of oak. I left a thin layer of this on the top of the Padauk because I though it might be attractive. I knew that if I did not like it, I could part it off later. (See Figure 85.)

Figure 85. I left a thin layer of this on the top of the Padauk because I though it might be attractive. I knew that if I did not like it, I could part it off later.

Shaping the Lid to the Bottom

Put the lid on the bottom of the box now. Hold the lid in place with your tailstock. (See Figure 86.) Here I am using my tailstock as a large flat dead center. Notice that there is no live center. I am just using the tailstock. There is almost no pressure on the lid, so it does not heat up. Use your bowl gouge to blend both sides of the box together. Do most of your final shaping at this time.

Figure 86. Put the lid on the bottom of the box now. Hold the lid in place with your tailstock.

Use a pencil to mark the parting off point. (See Figure 87.) Use your bowl gouge to shape the bottom of the box. (See Figure 88.) Use a skew to flatten the top of the box. (See Figure 89.) You will notice that the fingers of my left hand are in a slightly awkward position. This is because I am taking the photograph at the same time that I am making the cut. The top must be flat to accept the inlay veneer. Sand the entire box at this time. (See Figure 90.) Apply finish. (See Figure 91.)

Figure 87. Use a pencil to mark the parting off point.

Figure 88. Use your bowl gouge to shape the bottom of the box.

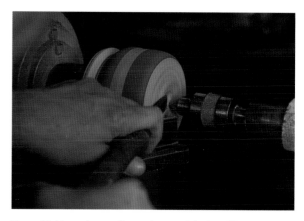

Figure 89. Use a skew to flatten the top of the box. The top must be flat to accept the inlay veneer.

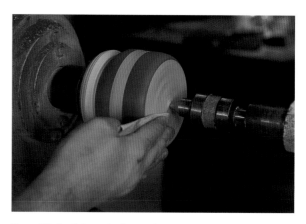

Figure 90. Sand the entire box at this time.

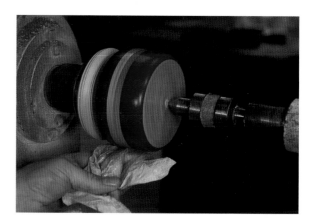

Figure 91. Apply finish. Be sure to use a paper towel and not a cloth. Cloth is very dangerous if the lathe grabs it.

Adding the Veneer

Cutting the Veneer Rebate

You have completed the regular work of making a box, except for parting off the bottom, sanding the bottom, and applying finish. Now you are ready to inlay the veneer. Start by laying down about six layers of duct tape around the joint of the box. (See Figure 92.) We do not want the lid to spin while cutting the inlay rebate. This would cause the lid to fit too loose and would mar the inside of the lid with a burn mark.

Figure 94. Transfer the diameter of the inlay measurement to the box lid. If the pencil circle is not exact, then draw a new one. .

Figure 92. You are ready to inlay the veneer. Start by laying down about six layers of duct tape around the joint of the box. You do not want the lid to spin while cutting the inlay rebate.

Use a sharp skew to make a straight in cut, just barely inside the pencil mark. (See Figures 95-96.) Use your skew to cut the rebate the exact thickness of the veneer. The depth of the cut needs to be accurate.

Use your calipers to measure the exact diameter of the inlay. (See Figure 93.) Lock the calipers in place once your have the correct measurement. Center the calipers on the top of the bowl, and make a test mark with a pencil. Turn the lathe on and make a light pencil circle. Turn the lathe off and reposition your calipers. If the pencil circle is not exact, then draw a new one. Adjust the pencil circle until the measurement is exact. (See Figure 94.) If you look at Figure 94 closely, you can tell that I have erased previous pencil circles.

Figure 95. Use a sharp skew to make a straight in cut, just barley inside the pencil mark.

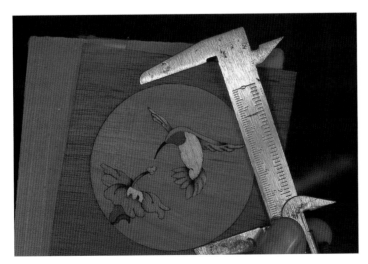

Figure 93. Use your calipers to measure the exact diameter of the inlay.

Figure 96. Use your skew to cut the rebate to the exact thickness of the veneer.

Veneers are very thin. The veneer that I used was thirty thousandths of an inch thick. This is the same thickness of six pages of regular white paper. The veneer needs to sit perfectly in the rebate because you cannot sand very much off the veneer without destroying it.

Test fit the veneer. (See Figure 97.) Your circle rebate should be a little bit too small. Use your skew to barely make the circle a little larger. Test fit again. Do this until you have a perfect fit. **The rebate must be flat and smooth. Any imperfections will show through the veneer once it is glued and dried**. I have the wrong side of the veneer facing out for photographic purposes. In real life you have the paper side of the veneer facing out. (See Figure 97.)

Figure 97. Test fit the veneer. Your circle rebate should be a little bit too small. Use your skew to make the circle slightly larger. Test fit again. Do this until you have a perfect fit.

Gluing the Veneer

You are now ready to glue the veneer. There are several items that you need to get in advance of the gluing process. You need the following items: wax paper (it does not show up well in the photograph), closed cell foam pad, a square of plywood, and glue. (See Figure 98.)

Figure 98. Arrange the items you need in advance of the gluing process.

Apply a drop of yellow glue to the side of the veneer that does not have paper on it. Spread the glue evenly. Try not to have excess glue. Now place a drop of glue into the rebate of the lid. Spread the glue around. Align the grain of the veneer with the grain of the lid. Carefully position the veneer into the rebate. (See Figure 99.) Place a piece of wax paper over the veneer. (See Figure 100.) Position the closed cell foam over the wax paper. (See Figure 101.) The foam will apply even pressure to the veneer. Now place a piece of plywood over the foam. Advance the tailstock forward so that it

applies pressure to the plywood, which will apply pressure to the foam. (See Figure 102.) This creates a nice even pressure to hold the veneer flat while the glue dries. Allow the glue to dry overnight.

Figure 99. Apply a drop of yellow glue to the side of the veneer that does not have paper on it. Spread the glue evenly. Try not to have excess glue.

Figure 100. Place a piece of wax paper over the veneer. This will keep the glue from going everywhere.

Figure 101. Position the closed cell foam over the wax paper. This will apply even pressure to the veneer as the glue sets.

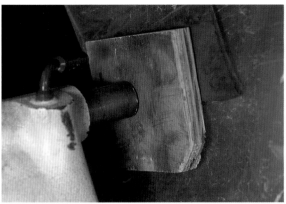

Figure 102. Place a piece of plywood over the foam. Advance the tailstock forward so that it applies pressure to the plywood, which will apply pressure to the foam.

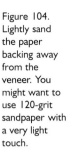

Figure 104. Lightly sand the paper backing away from the veneer. You might want to use 120-grit sandpaper with a very light touch.

Finishing the Veneer

Remove the tailstock, plywood, foam, and wax paper. You should have very little excess glue. Carefully sand away the excess glue, and blend the outside of the lid to the veneer. Be careful to not remove any thickness of the veneer in this process. You should be removing from the outside rim, not the veneer. (See Figure 103.)

Figure 105. Sand in the direction of the grain. Be very careful to remove very little of the veneer. It is very easy to sand through a veneer!! Sand to 400- to 800-grit sandpaper.

Final Touches

Use your skew or sandpaper to reduce the tenon on the bottom of the box. This will make the top slide on easily. Go slowly and carefully. You do not want to remove so much that you have a sloppy fit of the lid.

You are now ready to part off the bottom of the box. Use your thin parting tool. (See Figure 106.) I like to point my parting tool toward the tailstock so that I get a concave bottom. To me this makes a more attractive bottom than a flat bottom. Be careful not to cut a hole in the bottom of your bowl. Sand the bottom and apply finish by hand.

Figure 103. Carefully sand away the excess glue, and blend the outside of the lid to the veneer. Be careful to not remove any thickness of the veneer in this process. You should be removing from the outside rim only and not the veneer.

Now lightly sand the paper backing away from the veneer. You might want to use 120-grit sandpaper with a very light touch. (See Figure 104.) Stop the lathe often to see your progress. When most of the paper has been removed, move to 220-grit sandpaper to remove the final thickness of paper. Stop often to check your progress. When most of the paper has been removed with 220-grit sandpaper, turn the lathe off. Finish removing the last of the paper with hand sanding. Rub in the direction of the grain. Be very careful to remove very little of the veneer. It is very easy to sand through a veneer!! Sand to 400- to 800-grit sandpaper. Apply finish. (See Figure 105.)

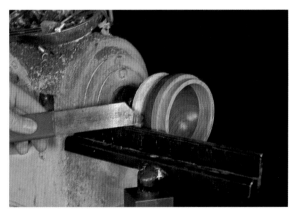

Figure 106. Use your thin parting tool to part off the bottom of the box.

I decided to remount the lid on a four jaw chuck to re-cut around the top. I had too much oak showing to be attractive. I used a skew to cut a "V" around the veneer and on the outside edge of the oak. (See Figure 107.) This made the oak ring stand out more and highlighted the hummingbird inlay. (See Figure 108.)

Figure 107. I remounted the lid on a four-jaw chuck to re-cut around the top so that I could take away some of the excess oak that I have showing. I used a skew to cut a "V" around the veneer and on the outside edge of the oak.

Figure 108. The oak ring made the hummingbird inlay stand out better.

Conclusion

Congratulations! You have just created a beautiful inlaid box. You have mastered a lot of turning and inlaying skills in this project. This is a beautiful project that will be admired by many and enjoyed by your loved ones for years to come.

Oval Inlay into a Platter

Inlaying veneers into platters is a natural use of veneer inlays. Platters by themselves are beautiful and a great way to show your artistic abilities. Platters combined with veneer inlays can be a powerful artistic combination. They are fun to do and will give you a lot of pleasure.

Truus Beisterveld from The Netherlands sent me a beautiful ash platter that she had turned. This turned out to be a very nice joint project. Truus did the turning and I did the inlaying. I had posted a notice on my web site, http://www.woodturningplus.com, that I was looking for turners around the world to do joint projects with on this book. I was very pleased that Truus wanted to work with me. She is one of The Netherlands's leading turners and the inventor of the CD top, which appeared in *Woodturning* magazine issue 88, June 2000, page 65.

Truus' platter arrived completed except that it did not have a finish, and a foot was still on the platter. The foot allowed me to re-chuck the platter. Being able to re-chuck the turning is a real advantage in a lot of situations. If you are inlaying a round inlay or an inlay band veneer, the remounting is vital. In this case I was doing an oval inlay on a regular lathe. I could not cut the entire inlay blank with the lathe; but it allowed me to flatten the platter, which was a big help.

Getting Started

The first step for me was to select the veneer that I wanted to inlay. (See Figure 109.) Choose a pretty inlay because you are going to be looking at it a lot.

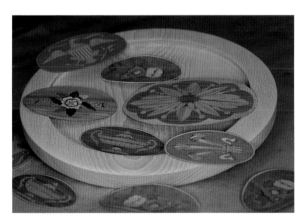

Figure 109. Choose a pretty inlay because you are going to be looking at it a lot.

Removing a Bad Cut

The bad rebate cut that I made was about thirty four thousands of an inch deep. To remove the bad rebate cut, I mounted the platter back on the lathe. This is where you are glad that you still have a means to remount a turning. I used my bowl gouge to cut a large flat circle in the center of the platter. I used a short straight edge to make sure that the center of the platter was flat. (See Figure 110.) I used pencil lines to mark where the wood stood proud. (See Figure 111.) I then very carefully use my bowl gouge to make this area flat. (See Figure 112.) I then feathered this circle all the way out to the edge of the platter. Next I sanded the inside of the platter with 220-grit sandpaper. This brought the platter back to nearly the same condition it was in when I received it.

Figure 110. I used a short, straight edge to make sure that the center of the platter was flat.

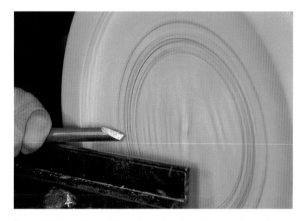

Figure 111. I used pencil lines to mark where the wood stood proud. I then very carefully used my bowl gouge to make this area flat.

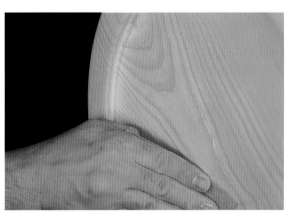

Figure 112. Next I sanded the inside of the platter with 220-grit sandpaper. This brought the platter back to nearly the same condition it was in when I received it.

Making Accurate Measurements

Successful inlays require very accurate measurements and cuts. Whenever possible I like to make the cuts on the lathe. Lathe cuts can be very easy and accurate. For the oval inlay I was able to make part of the oval cut, the central circle, on the lathe.

First I measured the narrow part of the diameter of the oval inlay using calipers. (See Figure 113.)

Figure 113. Using calipers, measure the narrow part of the oval inlay's diameter.

I transferred this measurement to a compass and drew the circle onto the center of the platter. (See Figure 114.) This did two things. First, it gave me the center of the platter and, second, it allowed me to cut the central circle on the lathe.

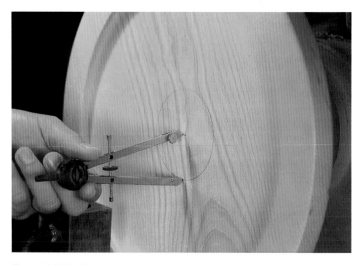

Figure 114. Transfer the diameter of the narrow part of the inlay to a compass, and draw the circle onto the center of the platter.

Next I carefully laid the oval inlay over the circle and traced the oval onto the platter. (See Figure 115.) Remember to have the untaped side of the inlay down. You will glue the untaped side of the inlay into the rebate. You now have the oval pattern of the inlay and the circular part drawn on the platter. Look at your pencil drawings. They should be perfect. If not, erase and do over.

Figure 115. Carefully place the oval inlay over the circle, and trace the oval onto the platter.

You can cut the circular part of the rebate on the lathe.

I used a very sharp skew to make a straight in cut into the platter at the pencil circle. (See Figure 116.) Your cut should be sharp and clean. The cut needs to go only about the depth of six pages of white paper. I then laid the skew flat on the tool rest and removed the thickness of the inlay. This cleared out the central circular part of the inlay rebate. (See Figure 117.)

Figure 116. Use a very sharp skew to make a straight in cut into the platter at the pencil circle. Your cut should be sharp and clean.

Figure 117. The cut only needs to go about the depth of six pages of white paper.

Correct Depth

Whenever possible, it best to take direct measurements. Measuring devices like tape measures, when used twice, give indirect measurements. To get a direct measurement of the thickness of the veneer compared to the thickness of the rebate, **I laid a**

piece of the veneer into the rebate to get a direct measurement. (See Figure 118.) A lot of circular veneers come to you as a square, and you have to remove the square part by breaking it free. The part that you break free is useful for making test measurements. Cut the rebate so that the veneer test stock lays flush with the edge.

Figure 120. Make small adjustments to the height of the bit with the vertical height adjustment.

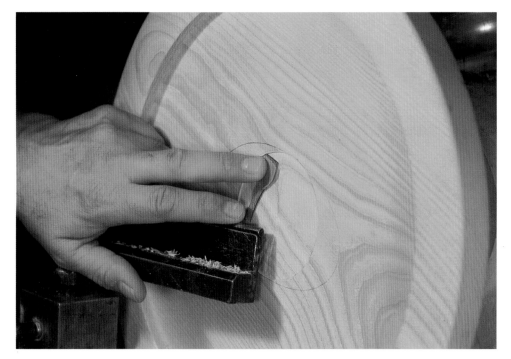

Figure 118. To get a direct measurement of the thickness of the veneer compared to the thickness of the rebate, lay a piece of the veneer into the rebate to get a direct measurement.

Setting the Depth of the Router

The second part of the rebate will be cut with a small laminate router. Use a flat 1/4-inch straight router bit. Insert the router bit and tighten firmly with the two wrenches that are provided. (See Figure 119.) Make small adjustments to the height of the bit with the vertical height adjustment. (See Figure 120.) Set the final depth by using the veneer inlay as a guide. (See Figure 121.) When making adjustments to a router, make sure that the router is unplugged.

Figure 121. Set the final depth by using the veneer inlay as a guide. When making adjustments with a router, make sure that the router is unplugged.

Figure 119. Use a flat 1/4-inch straight router bit. Insert the router bit, and tighten firmly with the two wrenches that are provided.

Applying the Veneer Inlay

Routing the Rebate

Carefully cut the rest of the rebate with the router. (See Figure 122.) Be sure to hold the router firmly with both hands. Have very good lighting so that you can see where you are cutting. I need magnification to be able to see the fine line of the pencil. Careful cutting can give you a very nicely cut rebate. (See Figure 123.) Test fit to make sure that the veneer fits snugly into the rebate. (See Figure 124.) Here I have the wrong side of the veneer up for photographic purposes. If the veneer does not fit in, mark the area that is too tight. Then very carefully remove a very small amount with the router.

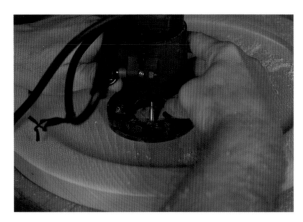

Figure 122. Carefully cut the rest of the rebate with the router. Be sure to hold the router firmly with both hands.

Figure 123. Careful cutting can give you a very nicely cut rebate.

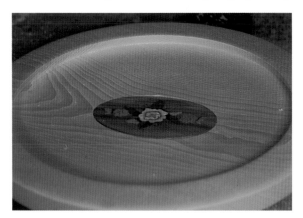

Figure 124. Test fit to make sure that the veneer fits snugly into the rebate.

Set Up for Gluing

Spend a couple of minutes getting everything ready for the glue-up. This will make the glue-up less stressful. You will need your glue, wax paper, a foam pad, a couple of scrap pieces of wood, and some wood clamps. (See Figure 125.)

Figure 125. Arrange the gluing supplies that you will need. These include: glue, wax paper, a foam pad, a couple of scrap pieces of wood, and some wood clamps.

Glue-up

When everything is prepared, the glue-up becomes easy. Place a dab of glue into the rebate. (See Figure 126.) Spread this around with your finger. (See Figure 127.) Be sure that you have an adequate even coat of yellow glue. Place the veneer into the rebate, making sure that the tape side of the veneer is up. (See Figure 128.) Wipe away excess glue. Place wax paper over the veneer. (See Figure 129.) Next, place a closed cell foam pad over the wax paper. (See Figure 130.) This pad will transfer even pressure to the entire inlay. Now place a square piece of plywood onto the foam. (See Figure 131.) Lay a piece of plywood across this square piece and apply pressure with four wood clamps. (See Figure 132.) Allow this glue to set up over night.

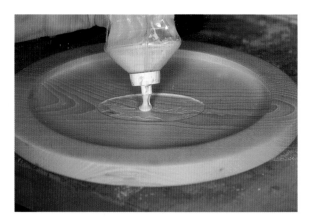

Figure 126. Place a dab of glue into the rebate.

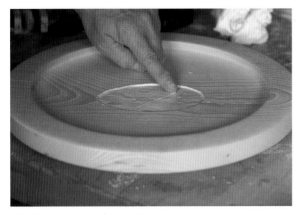

Figure 127. Spread the glue around with your finger. Be sure that you have an adequate, even coat of yellow glue.

Figure 128. Place the veneer into the rebate; make sure that the tape side of the veneer is up. Wipe away excess glue.

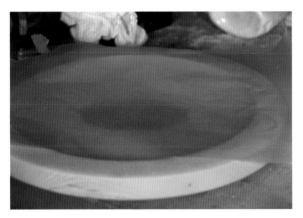

Figure 129. Place wax paper over the veneer.

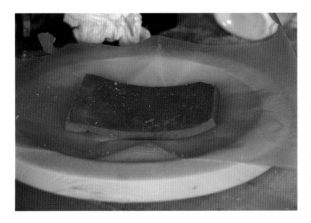

Figure 130. Place a close cell foam pad over the wax paper. This pad will transfer even pressure to the entire inlay.

Figure 131. Place a square piece of plywood onto the foam.

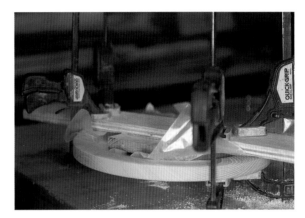

Figure 132. Lay a piece of plywood across this square piece, and apply pressure with four wood clamps. Allow this glue to set up overnight.

An alternate way to apply pressure to the glue-up is to remount the plate on the 4-jaw chuck and apply pressure with the tailstock. (See Figure 133.) This is my preferred method for applying pressure to the veneer.

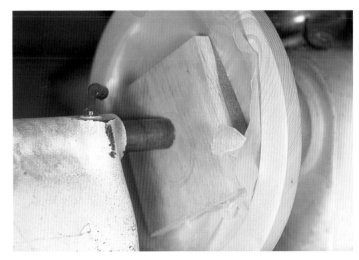

Figure 133. An alternate way to apply pressure to the glue-up is to remount the plate on the 4-jaw chuck and apply pressure with the tailstock. This is my preferred method for applying pressure to the veneer.

Allow the yellow glue to dry for twenty-four hours. (See Figure 134.) Notice that the taped side of the veneer is up.

Figure 134. Allow the yellow glue to dry for twenty-four hours. Notice that the taped side of the veneer is up.

Sanding

In ideal veneer inlays, it is necessary to sand only enough to remove the paper that is on the top of the veneer. However, on this project it was necessary for me to sand quite a bit more. The bottom of the platter curved up toward the rim. To get an adequate thickness for the veneer rebate at the long end of the rebate, it was necessary for me to make a deeper cut at the short diameter of the rebate. I ended up having a deeper cut on the narrow part of the rebate.

Initially, I removed part of the thickness with 60-grit sandpaper and a random orbital sander. (See Figure 135.) This would have been my preferred choice for the job. However, the sander died shortly after I started; I had to resort to my air powered die grinder with a drum sander on it. (See Figure 136.) I removed the bulk of the excess wood with this tool. I then completed the job using a hand sanding pad and 60-grit sandpaper. (See Figure 137.) I progressed to 120-grit sandpaper, staying off the veneer. When you get to 120-grit sandpaper, you can very carefully start removing the paper from the veneer. (See Figure 138.) I went all the way to 400-grit sandpaper. (See Figure 139.) Go slowly, and be patient. Like all other steps in this project, the sanding process is very important.

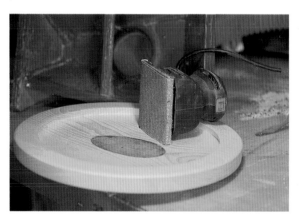

Figure 135. Initially I removed part of the thickness with 60-grit sandpaper and a random orbital sander.

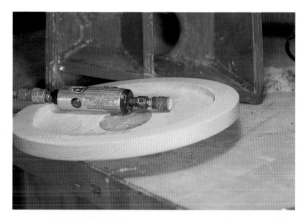

Figure 136. The sander died shortly after I started, so I had to resort to my air powered die grinder with a drum sander on it.

Figure 137. Complete the sanding job using a hand sanding pad and 60-grit sandpaper.

Figure 138. When you get to 120-grit sandpaper, you can very carefully start removing the paper from the veneer.

Figure 139. Sand all the way to 400-grit sandpaper. Go slowly and be patient. Like all other steps in this project, the sanding process is very important.

Applying Finish

I like to use Deft cellulose finish because it looks good and dries fast. It is very important that you use good ventilation and a good chemical respirator when using lacquer. I use Deft cellulose diluted 50/50 with lacquer thinner. For this project I sprayed it on with an inexpensive spray gun. (See Figure 140.) I sprayed on a thin protective coat and let it dry overnight because it was quitting time.

Figure 140. I use Deft cellulose diluted 50/50 with lacquer thinner. For this project, I sprayed it on with an inexpensive spray gun.

Finishing the Bottom

I returned the platter to the lathe to re-finish the bottom. I had chucked the platter up several times and the foot was now showing several marks. I used the jumbo jaws for my 4-jaw chuck. I did not want to make any artistic change to Truus's platter. I only wanted to clean up the marks that I had made. I made a very gentle skew cut to redefine the foot, and then I sanded to 400-grit sandpaper. (See Figure 141.) I then returned the platter to my worktable and finished spraying on my finish. You can just barely see part of the spray nozzle in the top left corner of the photograph. (See Figure 142.)

Figure 141. Return the platter on the lathe to re-finish the bottom.

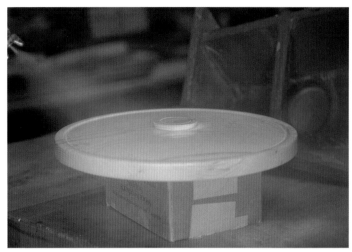

Figure 142. I then returned the platter to my worktable and completed spraying on my finish. You can barely see part of the spray nozzle in the top left corner of the photo.

Conclusion

Congratulations, you have learned how to inlay a beautiful platter with a veneer inlay. Your will be able to increase the beauty of your work and greatly increase the marketability of your turnings. I can guarantee that people will gather around your inlaid turnings whether you are at craft fairs or turning symposiums.

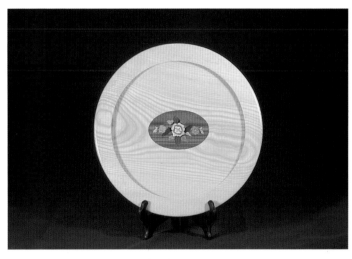

Figure 143. The completed platter.

Banding a Beautiful Bowl Rim

Placing a veneer band around a beautiful bowl can make that bowl look extraordinary. What was once a pretty bowl becomes a piece of art. Learning how to place a veneer band is not difficult. It does take a little bit of time. But the results far exceed the difficulty. Once you achieve basic wood turning ability, this may be the next most important learning goal.

Like all other veneer work, the wood must be dry. This is to prevent future difficulty with the wood cracking and warping. Dry wood has already gone through most of its changes. The chances of dry wood making significant dimensional changes is small compared to wet (green) wood.

For this project we will be making a segmented bowl and placing a veneer band around the rim. This will give you the opportunity to learn a lot about segmented turning and veneer rim banding in the same project.

The Project

The project is a segmented bowl made from seven rings and a solid base of Padauk. (See Figure 144.) Six of the rings are made from maple, and the top ring is made from Padauk. This means that the top and the bottom will be red and the middle will be white. This makes a nice color contrast. The red Padauk makes a nice "palette" to lay the veneer into. It is like you are painting, the Padauk is your palette, and the veneer is your paint.

Figure 145. A life-size drawing is actually quite simple to make. First choose the prettiest bowl profile that you have done.

A life-sized drawing is actually quite simple to make. (Once you figure out how to do it, that is. It took me *only* six weeks to figure it out. Yeah, I know, I am slow sometimes.) First choose the prettiest bowl profile that you have done. (See Figure 145.) Then make a tracing jig that will allow you to follow the contour of the bowl. (See Figure 146.) Get a friend to help you hold the bowl while you trace the profile. (See Figure 147.) Make several copies of this drawing. On one of the copies, draw the thickness of the rings that you will be using. Adjust the thickness of the top three rings to make the height come out correctly. (See Figure 148.) Draw in the contrasting colors of the rings and the veneer inlay rim.

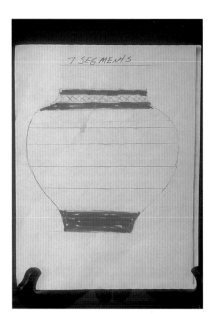

Figure 144. The project is a segmented bowl made from seven rings and a solid base of Padauk.

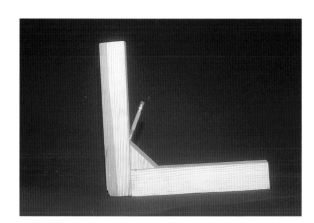

Figure 146. Make a tracing jig that will allow you to follow the contour of the bowl.

Figure 147. Get a friend to help you hold the bowl while you trace the contour.

Getting Started

I find it helpful to have a drawing of the segmented project before I start. Start with a bowl shape that you really like. (See Figure 145.) If I just "wing it," my results are hit-or-miss. When I have a "blue print" to go by, my work is much simpler and much more organized.

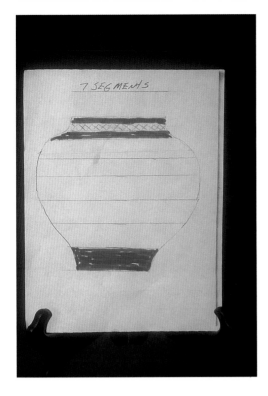

Figure 148. Draw the thickness of the rings that you will be using. Adjust the thickness of the top three rings to make the height come out correctly.

Figure 150. Accurate segments are easy to cut on a shooting board. Be sure to have earmuffs and a good face shield.

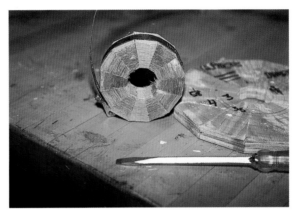

Figure 151. Make a test ring, and pull it together with a hose clamp. There should be no gaps.

Making Rings

From my drawing, I knew that I needed seven rings. Six of the rings would be maple, and one ring would be Padauk. I decided that I wanted my rings to be made of twelve segments. Twelve segments make a nice ring, one that is quick and easy to make. This miter angle for a twelve segment bowl is fifteen degrees. Prepare the equipment and materials that you need to make ring segments. In Figure 149, I have my drawing, hose clamps, and my segment size indicator. The segment size indicator is homemade. I have measured different size circles off my drawing. I transfer this measurement to the segment size indicator to determine the size of the segments. This allows me to make the correct size rings without guesswork.

Cutting the Segments

Use your segment size indicator to determine how wide a segment you need to cut. Then cut twelve segments to make that ring. Keep the segments in their separate piles. Adjust your "shooting board" for the next set of segments and make the cuts. Do this for all of the rings.

Gluing the Segments

Gluing the segments will be quick and easy if you have made the correct preparations. Organize your worktable so that you can work easily without clutter. Lay a piece of wax paper or aluminum foil on the table to keep glue from getting on the table. (See Figure 152.) I used aluminum foil here because I found it in my shop before I found the wax paper. Both work equally well.

Figure 149. Arrange the items that you need to construct segments.

The next step is to calibrate the "shooting board" that I use to cut the angled segments. (See Figure 150.) The last time I used the board I had cut twenty-four segments for a ring. I readjusted the guide to get close to the correct angle. I then made test cuts and minor adjustments until I got a perfect cut. (See Figure 151.) You will notice in Figure 151 that I have alternated the red top with the black and white bottom when putting the ring together. This eliminates any tilt of the blade error if there is one. Hopefully you have your blade set to a perfect 90 degrees.

Figure 152. Use a paper plate to act as a gluing area. Use a segment to spread the glue over the paper plate. Then coat a thin layer of glue onto both edges of the segment, and lay it onto the aluminum foil or wax paper.

Use a paper plate to act as a gluing area. Use a segment to spread the glue over the paper plate. Then coat a thin layer of glue onto both edges of the segment and lay it onto the aluminum foil or wax paper. Do this with the second segment. Press the first and second segments lightly together. Continue to do this until all twelve segments have been glued and assembled into a ring.

Place a hose clamp around the twelve glued segments. (See Figure 153.) Very lightly tighten the hose clamp using a screwdriver. Adjust the segments so that they are all even and flat on the table. Tighten the hose clamp. This will express some glue from each joint. Do not tighten so much that you express all the glue from the joint. This would make a weak glue joint. Wipe excess glue from the top and bottom of the ring using a paper towel. Using yellow glue, it is necessary to let the hose clamp remain in place for at least fifteen minutes.

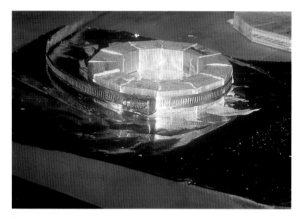

Figure 153. Place a hose clamp around the twelve glued segments. Wipe excess glue from the top and bottom of the ring using a paper towel. Using yellow glue, it is necessary to let the hose clamp remain in place for at least fifteen minutes.

While the first ring is setting, start preparing to glue the second ring. Lay out another piece of wax paper or aluminum foil. Arrange the segments, glue, and hose clamp. Start gluing and place a second hose clamp. About five hose clamps are all that you need. By the time that you get the fifth hose clamp on, you can remove and reuse the first hose clamp. (See Figure 154.) Here I have all seven rings glued up. Allow these rings to set up overnight.

Figure 154. You can glue-up all of your segments in one night. Allow these rings to set up overnight.

Thickness Sanding the Rings

Segmented turning requires extensive use of thickness sanding. The rings must be sanded flat and smooth on both sides. Also, the two flat sides must be parallel to each other. There are two easy ways to do this thickness sanding.

First, a dedicated thickness drum sander does an excellent job. It is very fast, smooth, and accurate. The only disadvantage is that it costs from eight hundred to one thousand dollars. If you are going to be doing a lot of segmented work, a drum thickness sander is well worth the money.

The second technique is to use your lathe as a thickness sander. You can make a sanding disc to go on your lathe and handhold the ring against the sanding disc. (See Figure 155.)

Figure 155. You can make a sanding disc to go on your lathe and handhold the ring against the sanding disc.

A third alternative for a thickness sander is my machined steel thickness sander. (See Figure 156.) This consists of two 3/8-inch round steel plates with a Morse #2 taper machined on the end. This will sand the rings flat and parallel. In addition, the single Morse taper plate is used as a glue press for gluing up segments. (See Figures 157 to 160.) I sell the single plate for $170, and both plates for $320.

Sand the rings flat and parallel. (See Figure 156.) Also sand the rings to the thickness that you desire. (See Figure 156.) A thousand dollar drum thickness sander *is* faster than my $320 sander. Sand all of your rings at one time because you will be using your lathe later as a glue press.

Figure 156. My machined steel thickness sander is a nice way to thickness sand your rings. By using a second pressure plate, you can make the sides parallel to each other.

Lathe Glue Press

Use your lathe as a glue press. Start by mounting a 3/4-inch thick by 3 1/2-inch square piece of plywood on your faceplate. (See Figure 157.) Make sure that the screws of the faceplate do not go through the plywood. Now glue a 3/4-inch thick by 3 1/2-inch square piece of Padauk onto the plywood mounting square. (See Figure 157.) Do this by putting a dab of yellow glue onto the Padauk. Then push the glue against the plywood and make circular motions to spread the glue evenly. Check to make sure that both surfaces are covered. Then square the two pieces up and apply pressure with the Morse tape pressure plate. (See Figure 157.) Allow this glue to set for at least fifteen minutes.

Figure 157. The pressure plate makes using your lathe as a glue press easy.

Stacking Rings

You will stack four rings that get progressively larger. A new ring can be added about every fifteen minutes. To stack ring #1, remove the Morse Taper Pressure Plate. Add glue to the ring segment. Put the ring against the Padauk base and rotate to spread the glue. Center the ring #1 and apply pressure with the Morse taper pressure plate. Allow this to set for at least thirty minutes. In this case, I let it set overnight, because it was bedtime. Therefore I turned it round the next day before adding any more segments. (See Figure 158.)

Figure 158. Glue four rings that progressively get larger.

Add ring #3 in the same manner. Be sure to allow the yellow glue to set for at least fifteen minutes before you attempt to add another ring. (See Figure 159.) Apply pressure to the centered ring using the Morse taper pressure plate. Wipe off excess glue with a paper towel. Do not let it drip on your lathe. Continue stacking segments this way until you reach your maximum diameter of the bowl. (See Figure 160.) Allow these segments to set up overnight before turning.

Figure 159. Be sure to allow the yellow glue to set for at least thirty minutes before you attempt to add another ring. Apply pressure to the centered ring using the Morse taper pressure plate. Wipe off excess glue with a paper towel.

Figure 160. Continue stacking segments this way until you reach your maximum diameter of the bowl. Allow these segments to set up overnight before turning.

Initial Turning of the Stack

Once the yellow glue has set for twelve hours, you are ready to do the initial turning. At this point, the bowl is wide open and it will be very easy for you to turn the inside of the bowl. Turning the inside of the bowl later when it has a small opening would be much more difficult.

Start off by determining the diameter of the base of the bowl. I used a set of calipers to measure the drawing that I made. (See Figure 161.) Set the gauge to be just a little bit bigger than the drawing. This will give you some sanding and finishing room. I used my bowl gouge to turn down the Padauk base until I had the desired measurement. (See Figure 162.)

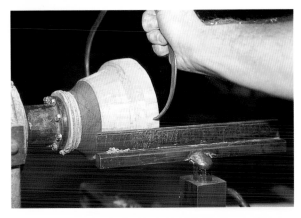

Figure 163. Measure the diameter at the widest segment. Turn the segment to this diameter.

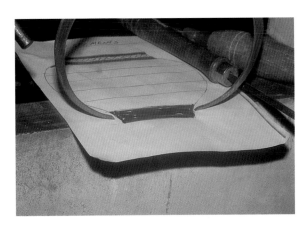

Figure 161. Determine the diameter of the base of the bowl using a set of calipers to measure the drawing that you made.

Figure 164. Use your bowl gouge to blend together the entire outside surface.

Figure 162. Set the gauge to be just a little bit bigger than the drawing. This will give you some sanding and finishing room.

Figure 165. Use the side of your bowl gouge to make a smooth, shear cut so that all external surfaces blend into a smooth, continuous form.

Next measure the diameter at the widest segment, the fourth segment. Turn the segment to this diameter. (See Figure 163.) Then use your bowl gouge to blend together the entire outside surface. (See Figure 164.) Use the side of your bowl gouge to make a smooth shear cut so that all external surfaces blend into a smooth continuous form. (See Figure 165.)

Turning the Inside

Turning the inside now while it is open will make the job much easier. Place a tool rest deep into the bowl. The closer the tool rest is to the work area the better. (See Figure 166.) I started off using my bowl gouge to rough out the inside. (See Figure 167.) I finished the inside work using a large round nose scraper. Scrapers work very well for this job. They give large beautiful shavings and a very smooth finish.

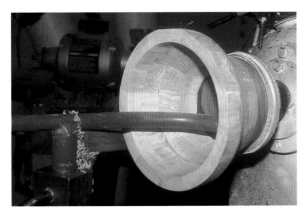

Figure 166. Turn the inside now while it is open. Position your tool rest as close as you can to the cutting area.

Figure 167. Start off cutting the inside of the bowl with your bowl gouge. Finish the inside work using a large round nose scraper.

Sanding the Inside

Sand the inside at this time. (See Figure 168.) Sanding now is much easier than later when the hole is small and the access is limited. Sand all the way to your final grit, which should be between 220 and 400-grit sandpaper.

Figure 169. Add the top segments one at a time.

Figure 168. Sand the inside at this time, while it is still open and easy to reach.

Adding Final Segments

Add the final segments to the top of the bowl. (See Figures 169 and 170.) Add glue to the segment and rotate the segment on the bowl. This will spread the glue evenly. Center the ring and hold it in place for fifteen minutes with the Morse taper faceplate. (See Figure 170.) Continue adding segments this way until all ring segments are in place. (See Figure 170.) Allow the yellow glue to set for twenty-four hours.

Figure 170. Add the final segment to the top of the bowl, and allow the yellow glue to set overnight.

Shaping the Outside

Put a live center into your tailstock. Cut a circular piece of plywood to go onto the end of the bowl to support the tailstock end. This is not glued to the bowl. (See Figure 171.) It just applies pressure to support the free end. Use your bowl gouge to shape the outside of the bowl.

Use your calipers to determine the diameter of the top of the bowl at the headstock end. Reduce the diameter to the desired width. Then blend together all the segments of the bowl. (See Figure 171.) Use the side of your bowl gouge to make very fine final shear cuts to the outside of the bowl. (See Figure 172.)

Figure 173. The round nose scraper is a safe way to cut the inside of the bowl with a small opening.

Figure 171. Put a live center into your tailstock. Cut a circular piece of plywood to go onto the end of the bowl to support the tailstock end.

Figure 172. Reduce the diameter to the desired width. Then blend together all segments of the bowl. Use the side of your bowl gouge to make very fine final shear cuts to the outside of the bowl.

Finishing the Inside of the Bowl

The easiest way to finish cut the rings of the top is to cut each ring after you have glued it on. However, you might not want to wait that long to glue on the next segment. Yet, be aware that if you have to finish cut all three smaller rings' interiors together, you will find it a little harder to reach up inside the bowl. You can use your bowl gouge or a round nose scrapper. (See Figure 173.) The scraper works very nicely and is the safest way to go. Take your time and do a very careful cutting job. Check the wall thickness often with thickness calipers. Be sure that you tool is sharp and that your lathe speed is not too high. I did my internal cutting at 500 RPM. This is a fairly slow speed and I did not want to break the bowl by putting too much vibration stress on it.

Final Sanding

Do the final sanding of the bowl at this time. Blend out any uneven spots with 80-grit sandpaper. (See Figure 174.) Cut these sanding marks out with 120-grit sandpaper. (See Figure 175.) Sand to your final grit, which should be at least 400-grit sandpaper. (See Figure 176.)

Figure 174. Do the final sanding of the bowl at this time. Blend out any uneven spots with 80-grit sandpaper.

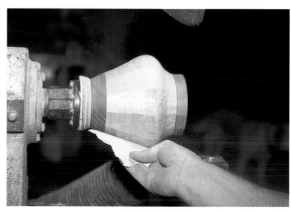

Figure 175. Cut sanding marks out with the next-grit sandpaper.

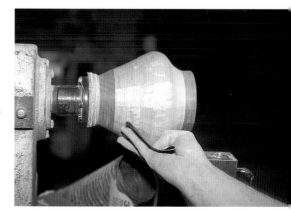

Figure 176. Sand to your final grit, which should be at least 400-grit sandpaper.

Inlaying a Veneer Rim

Inspect your supply of veneer strips and choose a veneer that you like. (See Figure 177.) It must go with the bowl and it must be the correct size for the area where you want to place it. You might want to make pencil marks where you want the veneer trim to go.

Figure 177. Choose a veneer that you like. It must go with the bowl and it must be the correct size for the area where you want to place it.

Use a very sharp skew to make a straight in cut just inside both pencil marks. Place the veneer test strip up against the marks. It should be just a little bit too small for the veneer to fit into. (See Figure 178.) Widen the test cut just enough so that the strip will tightly fit in. Check the fit again. It should be perfect. (See Figure 179.) Now use your skew to cut the rebate deep enough so that the veneer will rest flush in the rebate. Test the fit. It should be snug and the veneer should be flush with the top of the rebate. Take your time making this cut. Precision is important. People are going to look at your tight fit. Sand off any wood fibers that may remain. (See Figure 180.)

Figure 178. Use a very sharp skew to make a straight in cut just inside both pencil marks.

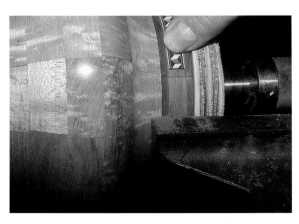

Figure 179. Place the veneer test strip up against the marks. It should be just a little bit too small for the veneer to fit into.

Figure 180. Sand off any wood fibers that may remain.

Cutting the Veneer Strip

Use a piece of string to measure around the rebate. Cut the veneer about one inch longer than this length. Look at your veneer and study the pattern on it. Decide where it will be easiest for you to line up the joint so that the pattern matches.

Doing a Test Fit

Place the veneer strip into the channel. Work it into the rebate all the way around. There should be extra veneer that overlaps at the ends. Use a sharp utility knife or a razor blade to cut through both layers of the overlap! This is important! If you cut through both layers you will have a perfect match.

Inlaying with Cyanoacrylic Glue

Place the veneer into the rebate and add a little cyanoacrylic glue to this small area. Add accelerator if your glue requires it. (See Figure 181.) The accelerator will quickly tack down the first end.

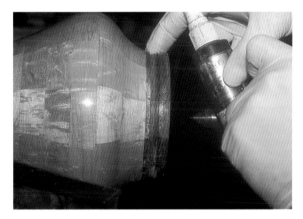

Figure 181. Place the veneer into the rebate, and add a little glue to this small area. Add accelerator if your glue requires it.

Now lay more veneer into the rebate where you have just added glue. Press this part of the veneer firmly into the rebate. (See Figure 182.) Add more cyanoacrylic glue and lay the next section down. (See Figure 183.) Press this section into the rebate and lock with accelerator. (See Figure 184.) Make sure that the veneer is glued in place well at the ends.

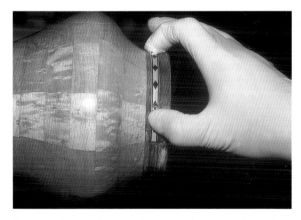

Figure 182. The accelerator will quickly tack down the first end. Now lay more veneer into the rebate where you have just added glue. Press this part of the veneer firmly into the rebate.

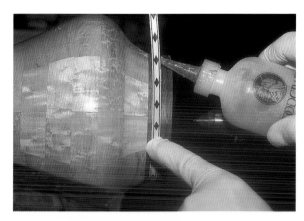

Figure 183. Add more cyanoacrylic glue and lay the next section down.

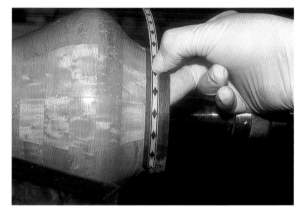

Figure 184. Press this section into the rebate and lock with accelerator.

If the veneer strip has stretched a small amount, you may need to trim a minute amount from the end of the veneer with a razor blade. (See Figure 185.)

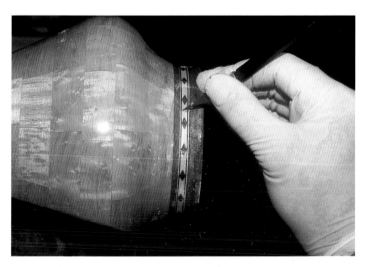

Figure 185. If the veneer strip has stretched a little bit, you may need to trim a minute amount from the end of the veneer with a razor blade.

Finishing the Veneer

The veneer should be flat with the surface of the bowl. If you make an error, it is better to make the rebate a little too deep. Make the surfaces of the bowl flush to the veneer with your bowl gouge. (See Figure 186.) Do not touch the veneer with the bowl gouge.

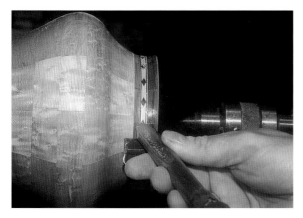

Figure 186. The veneer should be flat with the surface of the bowl. If you make an error, it is better to make the rebate a little too deep. Make the surfaces of the bowl flush to the veneer with your bowl gouge.

Sand the area smooth using 120-grit sandpaper on each side of the veneer. (See Figure 187.) Do not touch the veneer with 120-grit sandpaper. You can sand through it in just a few seconds. Sand the veneer and the adjacent area with 220-grit sandpaper. (See Figure 188.) Progress all the way up to at least 400-grit sandpaper. All of my sandpaper past 400-grit is black. I do not like black sandpaper. I am afraid that it will darken or mark light wood. So if your light colored sandpaper stops at 400-grit sandpaper, then you must stop at 400-grit sandpaper. Finish sanding the inside and outside at this time.

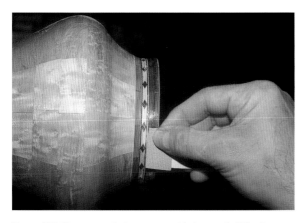

Figure 187. Do not touch the veneer with the rough 120-grit sandpaper. You can sand through it in just a few seconds. Sand the area smooth using 120-grit sandpaper on each side of the veneer.

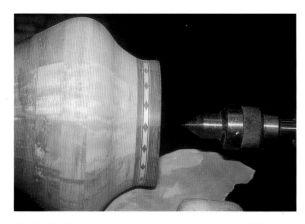

Figure 188. Sand the veneer and the adjacent area with 220-grit sandpaper.

Applying Finish

I believe that your turning should have a nice finish on it when it comes off the lathe. If you want a higher gloss, you can do some additional spraying later. But straight off the lathe it should look good. I use a 50/50 mixture of Deft cellulose diluted with lacquer thinner. Apply with a paper towel. (See Figure 189.) Have the lathe turning at a slow speed as you apply. Wipe it on and even it out with the "wet" paper towel. After you have wetted the bowl, wipe the excess off with your wet paper towel in about thirty seconds. Allow it to dry about thirty seconds between applications. (See Figure 190.) If it takes longer than this to dry then the mix is too thick, or you are putting in on too thick. This is a thin application technique. Apply four to twenty coats depending on what you like and how bored you can stand to be. I usually quit when my paper towel wears out.

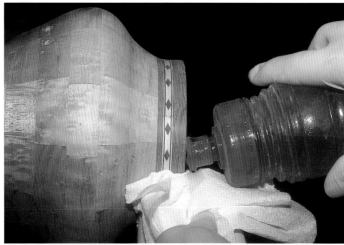

Figure 189. Apply your finish while it is still on the lathe.

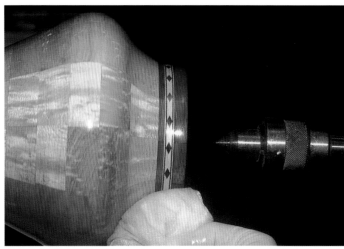

Figure 190. Allow the lacquer finish to soak for about thirty seconds, and then wipe it off with the same paper towel that you used to apply it.

Parting Off

Use your bowl gouge to reduce the diameter of the plywood at the base. (See Figure 191.) Use a thin parting tool – I like the Chris Scott thin parting tool – to part off the base. (See Figure 192.) Slightly incline the tool toward the tailstock so that you make a concave cut. I do not like flat bases. This cut is more attractive to me. (See Figure 193.)

Figure 191. Use your bowl gouge to reduce the diameter of the plywood at the base.

Figure 192. Use a thin parting tool to part off the vase.

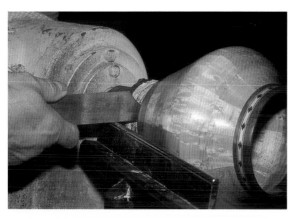

Figure 193. Hold the parting tool firmly with both hands.

Use your bowl gouge or skew to round over the corner of the base. Sand this part of the base while it is still on the lathe. (See Figure 194.) Apply finish to this area of the bowl. (See Figure 195.) You are now ready to do the final parting off of the bowl. Sand the bottom of the bowl by hand or with a round padded sanding disc. I really like the round padded sanding disc that is attached with hook and loop. (See Figure 196 – in this photograph I am sanding

the bottom of the project from the next chapter.) This is a very fast and easy way to finish the bottom.

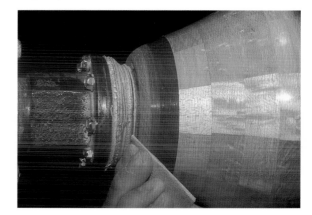

Figure 194. Sand the bottom of the vase before completing the parting cut.

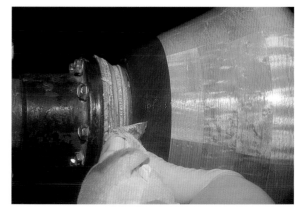

Figure 195. Apply finish to the bottom.

Figure 196. Sand the bottom smooth with a hook and loop sanding pad.

Conclusion

Congratulations! You have just completed a beautiful segmented bowl. In addition you have learned how to edge band the rim. With a little attention to detail your veneer inlay will stand up to the closest scrutiny. (See Figures 197-198.) This makes a very beautiful project that you and your loved ones will enjoy for years to come.

Figure 197. A well-done veneer inlay is beautiful and stands up to close inspection.

Figure 198. The finished vase.

Mixing Glass & Wood: Adding a Wood Base & Rim to a Glass Vase

We have heard that water and oil do not mix. But a vinegar (which is water based) and oil salad dressing can be quite good. Likewise, mixing wood and glass is not something the turner usually considers. However, mixing different art forms can sometimes lead to a new, unusual, and occasionally beautiful piece of art.

You can make a beautiful glass and wood turning by combining an inexpensive frosted glass vase with some beautiful turned and veneered wood. You can get beautiful frosted glass vases from arts and crafts stores. I got mine from Pier 1 Imports. (See Figure 199.)

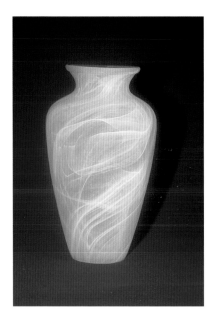

Figure 199. You can make a beautiful glass and wood turning by combining an inexpensive frosted glass vase with some beautiful turned and veneered wood.

Preparing a Base

Start by attaching a 3/4-inch thick, 3 1/2-inch square plywood piece to your base plate. Be sure that the wood screws do not come through the plywood. (See Figure 200.) Glue an attractive square turning blank to the plywood using yellow glue. I used a piece of 3/4-inch Padauk. (See Figure 200.) Apply even pressure to the turning blank using pressure from your tailstock. Allow this glue joint to set for twenty-four hours.

Figure 200. Start by attaching a 3/4-inch thick plywood 3 1/2-inch square to your base plate. Be sure that the wood screws do not come through the plywood.

Turning the Base

Rough turn the base once the glue has had adequate time to set. It is important to knock off the rough corners now because the joint between the glass and wood is not as strong as we would like it to be. Use your bowl gouge to knock off the corners. (See Figure 201.) Keep your lathe speed fairly low for this, about 500 RPM. Once the corners have been knocked off, you can increase the lathe speed and make a smooth round base. (See Figure 202.) The higher speed makes it easier to smooth cut and to make the chips fly. **The speed should not be over 1000 RPM, and it should never make your lathe vibrate.**

Figure 201. Rough turn the base once the glue has had adequate time to set. It is important to knock off the rough corners now because the joint between the glass and wood is not as strong as we would like it to be.

Figure 202. Keep your lathe speed fairly low for this, about 500 RPM. Once the corners have been knocked off, you can increase the lathe speed and make a smooth, round base.

Cutting a Rebate for the Glass Bottom

Cut a rebate in the base for the glass vase to fit into. The bottom of the glass vase was concave. To get a better glue joint I needed a concave bottom. But the most important reason that I had to cut a rebate in the base was that I needed the rebate to center the vase to the lathe and base plate.

Start by measuring the diameter of the base using a set of calipers. (See Figure 203.) Transfer this mark to the wood base. (See Figure 204.) Set the point closest to you to touch the wood and make a scratch. If the point on the other side lines up with the scratch you have made a correct transfer. If not, make an adjustment and make a second mark. You can also start off by making a pencil mark to help you get close, then make adjustments.

Figure 205. Use a very sharp skew to make a straight in cut.

Figure 203. Measure the diameter of the bottom of the glass vase.

Figure 206. Lay the skew flat onto the tool rest, and cut a shallow rebate.

Once you have the correct size rebate, use your bowl gouge to make it deeper. Also use the bowl gouge to cut the center projection that will fit into the concavity of the vase. (See Figure 207.) Test fit the glass vase to make sure that you have a very snug fit into the base. (See Figure 208.)

Figure 204. Transfer the diameter to the Padauk base.

Figure 207. Hollow a rebate that the vase will fit into nicely.

Figure 208. Test fit the glass vase to make sure that you have a very snug fit into the base.

Use a very sharp skew to make a straight in cut. (See Figure 205.) Lay the skew flat onto the tool rest and cut a shallow rebate. (See Figure 206.) This rebate is centered to the lathe and will help you seat the glass vase accurately. Test fit the glass vase to see that it fits into the rebate. Hopefully you have made the rebate a little bit too small and it will take you several attempts to get it big enough so that you have a snug fit. If the rebate is too big, immediately remove it and start over.

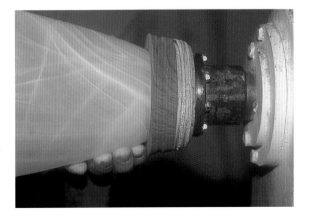

Glue Set Up

Some set up work is necessary to make gluing neat and easy. First the epoxy glue does not want to bond well to glazed glass. To give the glue something to cling to, it is necessary to scratch the vase bottom with a diamond stone. (See Figure 209.) This is the truing stone that I use to true up my grinding wheel. It has impregnated diamond in it. You could also use a diamond honing stone or a diamond fingernail file. Here I have scratched the entire bottom of the rim. I also scratched the entire top of the bowl rim at the same time so that I would not forget to do it at a later time.

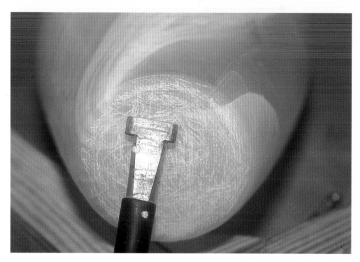

Figure 209. Scratch the bottom and top rim to give the glue a good surface to bond to.

Several other set up steps are necessary. First, get your epoxy glue out and something to mix it on. (See Figures 210 and 211.) Also, you will need to have a centering cone on your tailstock that will fit into the mouth of the vase. (See Figure 215.)

Figure 210. Use fastset epoxy glue for the bottom and top.

Figure 211. Use a paper plate of scrap wood to mix your glue.

Set the vase upside down. This will allow you to load the epoxy into the recess and have it sit still.

Gluing the Base

Mix the epoxy glue on a disposable pad. (See Figure 212.) Load epoxy onto the concave base of the upside down vase. This epoxy will sit still while you load epoxy onto the Padauk base. (See Figure 213.) This epoxy will want to run; so have a paper towel underneath it.

Figure 212. Mix the epoxy close to the headstock.

Figure 213. Load the epoxy into the bottom of the vase and onto the headstock base.

Now center the vase with its epoxy into the Padauk base rebate. There should be excess epoxy that expresses out of the joint. (See Figure 214.) Hold the vase in the center alignment using a large cone in your tailstock. (See Figure 215.) **When you remove the glass vase and the faceplate from the lathe, you must be very careful to support the vase so that you do not break the fragile joint!!!**

Figure 214. Position the vase, and hold it in place with a tailstock live center.

Figure 215. Allow the epoxy to set for at least three hours.

Set Up Time

How long does it take for "Five Minute Epoxy"™ to set up? Duuuh? Well, it is actually a good question. **Five-minute epoxy takes three hours to set up.** So leave this fragile joint alone for at least three hours. **When you remove the glass vase and the faceplate from the lathe, you must be very careful to support the vase so that you do not break the fragile joint!!!**

Making a Segmented Ring

Use a shooting board to make very accurate segment cuts. (See Figure 216.) To cut a twelve segmented ring, your miter gauge or your shooting board is set to fifteen degrees. Be sure to use a safety shield, earmuffs, and a respirator. Make test cuts using scrap wood. Pull the segments together with a hose clamp to see how close you have come. Make minor adjustments to your shooting board and make test cuts again. Continue doing this until you have a perfect ring with no gaps in it.

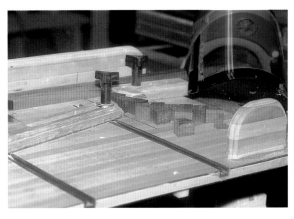

Figure 216. Use a shooting board to make very accurate segment cuts. Be sure to use a safety shield, earmuffs, and a respirator. Make test cuts using scrap wood.

Gluing the Segments

Create a working area with wax paper or aluminum foil. Place some yellow glue onto a paper plate. (See Figure 217.) Wipe the ends of the segment across the glue on the plate. This will spread a thin, even coat of glue across the ends of the segments. (See Figure 217.) Joint these segments together. (See Figure 218.) Build the entire ring this way.

Figure 217. Create a working area of wax paper or aluminum foil. Place some yellow glue into a paper plate or onto some wax paper.

Figure 218. Wipe the ends of the segment across the glue on the plate. This will spread a thin, even coat of glue across the ends of the segments.

Pull the segments together with very light pressure using a hose clamp. (See Figure 219.) Now adjust the individual segments to make sure that all are flat and that they are all flush with the outside circle. Then tighten the hose clamp. Do not over tighten. Remember, this is a glue joint; you do not want to tighten so much that all of the glue is expressed out. Allow the glue to set for twenty-four hours.

Figure 219. Pull the segments together with very light pressure using a hose clamp. Do not over tighten.

Thickness Sanding the Segment

Segmented work requires that the rings be sanded flat on both sides. This can be quickly and easily done with a thickness sander. If you do not have a thickness sander you can do it by making a disc sander to go on your lathe. (See Figure 220.) Sand both sides of the segmented ring. To make sure that the flat sides are parallel to each other, use a second Morse Taper face plate to flatten both sides to each other. (See Figure 221.) You may purchase a set from me if you wish. The final ring should be flat and smooth. (See Figure 222. Sorry about the ring, but my tailstock is in focus.)

Figure 220. Sand both sides of the segmented ring.

Figure 221. To make sure that the flat sides are parallel to each other, use a second Morse taper face plate to flatten both sides to each other.

Figure 222. The final ring should be flat and smooth.

Fitting the Top Ring

Use your calipers to measure the outside diameter of the rim of the glass vase. (See Figure 223.) Transfer this measurement to the ring, which is mounted, on your jumbo jaws. (See Figure 224.) You might want to do the initial transfer using a pencil mark. (See Figure 224.) Cut a shallow rebate using your skew. (See Figure 225.) Test the fit of the rim into this small rebate. When the fit is snug, deepen the rebate so that the wood fits around the rim. (See Figure 226.)

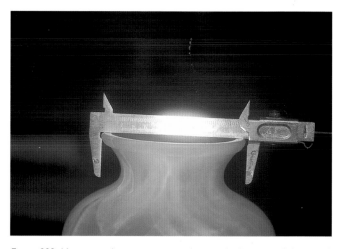

Figure 223. Use your calipers to measure the outside diameter of the rim of the glass vase.

Figure 224. Transfer the measurement to the segmented ring, which is mounted on your jumbo jaws.

50

Figure 225. Cut a shallow rebate using your skew. Test the fit of the rim into this small rebate.

Figure 226. When the fit is snug, deepen the rebate so that the wood fits around the rim.

Gluing the Top Ring

Glue the wood rim to the top of the vase. To do this there is a little preparation that will make the job easier. First, make sure that you have roughed up the surface of the top of the glass vase using a diamond cutter. Second, make sure that you have something like a Morse taper pressure plate in your tailstock. (This could be as simple as a piece of plywood that you use to apply pressure.) Third, have some wax paper available to put between the wood top and the Morse taper pressure plate.

Mix epoxy glue and apply some to both the rim of the glass vase and to the glue rebate. Place the

wood rim on the glass vase and then hold in place with the Morse taper pressure plate. (See Figure 227.) Fast set epoxy (five minute epoxy) takes three hours to set at room temperature. Do not disturb this joint before the three hours is up.

Figure 227. Mix epoxy glue, and apply some to both the rim of the glass vase and to the glue rebate. Place the wood rim on the glass vase and then hold in place with the Morse taper pressure plate.

Turning the Wood and Glass Vase

Remove the Morse taper pressure plate after the glue has set for three hours. Be careful to fully support the vase when you remove the pressure plate. Place a plywood circle against the top of the wood rim. (No glue is used – this is just for support) Bring your tailstock into place using a live center. Place the live center into the plywood with a small amount of pressure. (See Figure 228.) Do not use enough pressure to break the glass vase. Hand rotate the vase to make sure that it turns easily.

Figure 228. Place a plywood circle against the top of the wood rim. (No glue is used – this is just for support.) Bring your tailstock into place using a live center. Place the live center into the plywood with a small amount of pressure.

Set the speed of your lathe to about 500 RPM. **Be sure to put on a face shield!!!** You are turning glass and wood.

Do not attempt to cut the glass. You are only turning the wood. Use your bowl gouge to turn the outside of the wood rim. (See Figure 229.) **Cut slowly and gently.** Reduce the diameter of the rim so that it is no wider than the widest part of the base of the vase. Blend the bottom of the rim into the glass rim using a gentle taper. (See Figure 230.) Leave the rim a little wide at this time.

Figure 229. Use your bowl gouge and light pressure to turn the ring round.

Figures 230. Blend the bottom of the rim into the glass rim using a gentle taper. Leave the rim a little wide at this time.

Cutting the Inside of the Lid

To cut the inside of the rim, it is necessary to support the vase with a steady rest. My steady rest is homemade using steel and roller blade wheels. (See Figure 231.) You can make a very good steady rest using plywood. Place a layer of duct tape around the vase where the steady rest will be riding. This will help protect the glass from being marked by the rubber wheels. If you mark the glass with the rubber wheels, the marks will be quite difficult to remove.

Figure 231. To cut the inside of the rim, it is necessary to support the vase with a steady rest. My steady rest is homemade, using steel and roller blade wheels.

Have a friend support the vase when you remove the tailstock support and place the steady rest. Tighten the supporting wheels around the vase so that it is fully supported. Set your lathe speed to about 250 to 300 RPM.

Use your bowl gouge to make the initial cuts on the rim. Be gentle. Taper the rim toward the inside glass. A large round nose scraper makes a very nice finish cut. (See Figure 232.) Make slow, gentle cuts with the scraper to blend the wood into the glass. (See Figure 233.)

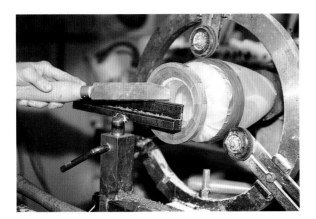

Figure 232. Use your bowl gouge to make the initial cuts on the rim. Be gentle. Taper the rim toward the inside glass. A large, round nose scraper makes a very nice finish cut.

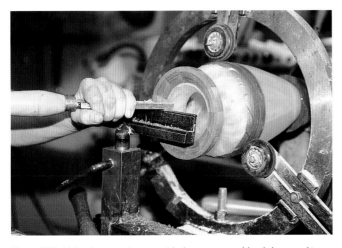

Figure 233. Make slow, gentle cuts with the scraper to blend the wood into the glass.

Finishing the Rim

Special attention is required for finishing the rim. Most likely the glass rim will not be perfectly flat to the lathe. This is because the glass was initially blown and then made into a cast so that duplicates could be made. It was not turned on your lathe! This will mean that you most likely will have to do some hand finishing of the joint where the glass and the wood meet.

Start finishing using course 80-grit sandpaper. (See Figure 234.) Take out all of the imperfections that you can with this rough paper. Use a sharp knife or palm chisel to cut away any thick epoxy glue. (See Figure 235.) Use a padded course-sanding disc on your electric drill to remove epoxy glue and blend the rim into the glass. (See Figure 236.) Take your time. This step may take an hour or two. I spent two hours hand finishing my rim.

Figure 234. Start finishing with course 80-grit sandpaper.

Figure 235. Take out all of the imperfections that you can with this rough paper. Use a sharp knife or palm chisel to cut away any thick epoxy glue.

Figure 236. Use a padded course-sanding disc on your electric drill to remove epoxy glue and blend the rim into the glass. Take your time. This step may take an hour or two.

Veneer Inlaying the Rim

A veneer inlay trim around the rim can really make the vase stand out. Choose a 1/4-inch wide veneer strip to go on the edge of the rim. (See Figure 237.) Choose one that is attractive to you. This is why we left the rim wide initially.

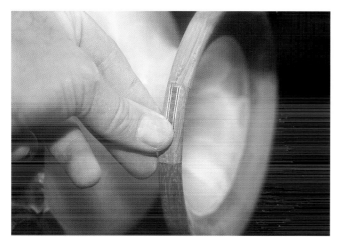

Figure 237. Choose an attractive inlay that will fit in your rim.

Use a sharp 1/4-inch round skew to cut your rebate. (See Figure 238.) You can use a sharp pencil to mark where the cuts need to be. Make your first cut straight into the rim. (See Figure 239.) Make your second cut just a little narrower than the veneer strip. (See Figure 240.) Check the measurement with your veneer test strip. (See Figure 241.) It should be a little too tight. Now re-cut just a little bit wider so that you get a perfectly tight fit. Test to make sure the fit is tight before you deepen the cut. Use your 1/4-inch round skew to cut the rebate. Make the rebate just slightly deeper than the veneer is thick.

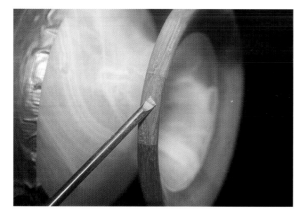

Figure 238. Use a sharp 1/4-inch round skew to cut your rebate.

Figure 239. Make your first cut straight into the rim.

Figure 240. Make your second cut just a little narrower than the veneer strip.

Figure 241. Check the measurement with your veneer test strip.

Cutting the Length of the Veneer

Use a piece of string to measure the circumference of the rebate. Cut a piece of veneer strip that is about 1/4 of an inch longer than the actual measurement. Place the veneer into the rebate. Make sure that it is fully seated all the way around. The ends of the veneer should overlap about 1/4 of an inch.

Inspect the overlap area and decide where you want your joint to be. If there is a repeating pattern, make the joint where it will be least noticeable. Use a sharp razor blade to cut through both layers of the overlap in one stroke. (See Figure 242.) **This double layer cut method will give you a perfect length for the veneer.**

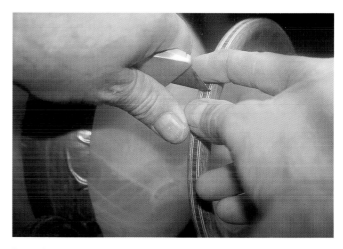

Figure 242. Use a sharp razor blade to cut through both layers of the overlap in one stroke.

Gluing the Veneer

Contact cement works well for this project. Shake the cement well, and place a small amount on the back of the veneer strip. (See Figure 243.) Use wax paper or a paper plate to keep from getting glue on your workbench. The original Dap Weldwood Contact Cement™ worked very well for me. (See Figure 244.)

Figure 243. Contact cement works well for this project. Shake the contact cement well, and place a small amount on the back of the veneer strip.

Figure 244. The Dap Weldwood™ Contact Cement worked very well for me.

Place a layer of contact cement into the rebate of the rim. A cotton swab makes an acceptable brush. (See Figure 245.) Allow both surfaces to dry until they are tacky. (Follow the instructions of the manufacturer.)

Figure 245. Place a layer of contact cement into the rebate of the rim. A cotton swab makes an acceptable brush.

When the glue is tacky on both surfaces, place one end of the veneer into the rebate. Make sure that it is fully seated. Use finger pressure to press it into place. (See Figure 246.) Slowly work more and more of the veneer into the rebate, being sure to fully press the veneer all the way down into the rebate. (See Figure 247.) Continue in this way until the veneer is full seated. Press both ends of the veneer down into the rebate. They should be perfectly matched and together.

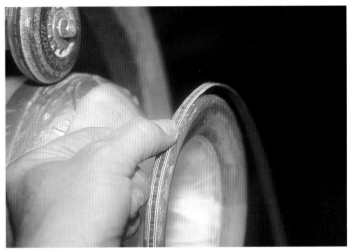

Figure 246. When the glue is tacky on both surfaces, place one end of the veneer into the rebate. Make sure that it is fully seated. Use finger pressure to press it into place.

Figure 247. Slowly work more and more of the veneer into the rebate, being sure to fully press the veneer all the way down into the rebate.

Finish Sanding the Edges Beside the Veneer

The edges beside the veneer should stand a little proud of the veneer. Carefully sand these edges down with 120-grit sandpaper. (See Figure 248.) The lathe should be running at about 200 RPM.

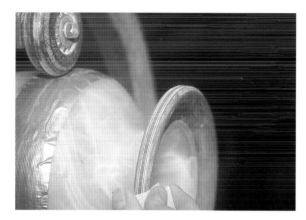

Figure 248. The edges beside the veneer should stand a little proud of the veneer. Carefully sand these edges down with 120-grit sandpaper.

Carefully round the edges over and blend the surfaces of the veneer and the rebate together with 180-grit sandpaper. (See Figure 249.) Be careful not to remove too much of the veneer. It is very thin. Sand all the way up to 400-grit sandpaper.

Figure 249. Carefully round the edges over and blend the surfaces of the veneer and the rebate together with 180-grit sandpaper.

Apply Finish to the Rim

Apply your favorite finish to the rim at this time. I use a mixture of Deft cellulose diluted 50/50 with lacquer thinner. (See Figures 250 and 251.) Notice that I have a 4-inch vacuum hose below my hand. You must be careful not to breathe the fumes of any of the solvents that are used in woodworking. Apply at least four coats of the lacquer to the rim while it is still on the lathe. (See Figure 251.)

Figure 250. Apply your favorite finish to the rim at this time. I used a mixture of Deft cellulose diluted 50/50 with lacquer thinner. (Notice that I have a 4-inch vacuum hose below my hand.)

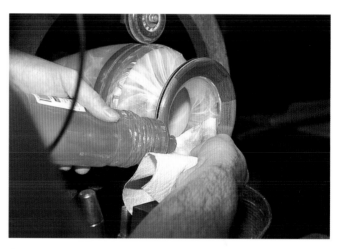

Figure 251. You must be careful not to breathe the fumes of any of the solvents that are used in woodworking. Apply at least four coats of the lacquer to the rim while it is still on the lathe.

Parting Off the Base

Place the live center cone into the throat of the vase to support the top of the vase. Do not apply too much pressure with the steady rest.

Remove the steady rest. I could not remove my steady rest easily so I moved it all the way toward the headstock. (See Figure 252.) Hand-rotate the vase to make sure that it turns freely.

Figure 252. Shape the foot of the vase with a bowl gouge and a light touch.

Turn the base down using your bowl gouge. (See Figure 252.) Blend the Padauk base to the glass very carefully. Some hand sanding may be required if the glass is not perfectly round. I spent about forty-five minutes hand sanding this area. Take your time. It is important that you have a smooth, pretty joint.

Use a thin parting tool to part off with. I like the Chris Scott thin parting tool. (See Figure 253.) Make a small parting cut at the junction between the Padauk and the plywood. This cut should only be about 1/2- to 1/4-inch deep. Now slightly round over the edge at the bottom with your skew. (See Figure 254.) Apply finish to the bottom and to the rest of the vase at this time. (See Figure 255.)

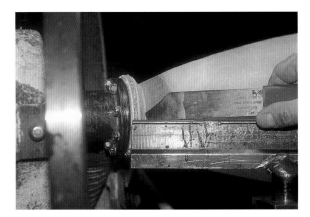

Figure 253. Use a thin parting tool to part the vase off.

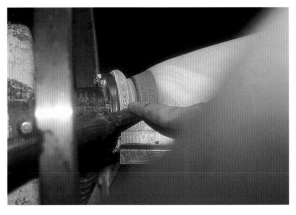

Figure 254. Make a small parting cut at the junction between the Padauk and the plywood. This cut should only be about 1/2 to 1/4-inch deep. Now slightly round over the edge at the bottom with your skew.

Figure 255. Apply finish to the bottom and the rest of the vase at this time.

Have a friend help support the vase as you part it off. Have the friend place one hand on the off switch so that you can turn the lathe off quickly. Make the parting cut slightly concave by pointing the tip of the parting tool slightly toward the tailstock. Sand the bottom of the base smooth with a pad and hook and loop sandpaper. (See Figure 256.) Hand-apply finish to the bottom of the vase.

Figure 256. Sand the bottom of the base smooth with a pad and hook and loop sandpaper. Hand-apply finish to the bottom of the vase.

Conclusion

Congratulations, you have just created a museum-quality piece of art. This is a piece of art that will be as welcome in art galleries as it is in your living room. (See Figure 257.) If you are an amateur turner, this will be a project that your family will enjoy for years to come.

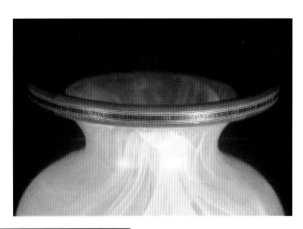

Above and left: Figure 257. Careful attention to detail will allow you to create a beautiful piece of art.

Inlaying a Flat Oval Veneer into a Round Vase

Inlaying an oval veneer into a beautiful vase can result in an impressive piece of art. However, it can be a little bit challenging. This is why I left this project for last. The project will require that you make very careful measurements and very careful cuts. But you have already acquired a lot of these skills, so this will not be anything too difficult.

I did this as a joint project with Lowell Converse. Lowell retired from the Air Force in 1987. He had turned years ago and then became serious about it a few years back. Lowell turned the vase in ash. (See Figure 258.) It was turned green with the pith in the middle. (See Figure 259.) That way, as the vase dried, it "warped" symmetrically around the center instead of becoming oval. It is often possible to do this without the piece cracking if it is thin enough. (See Figure 260.) Lowell's work can be found at the Village Artisans gallery in Yellow Springs, Ohio, or on his website: http://home.earthlink.net/~laconverse.

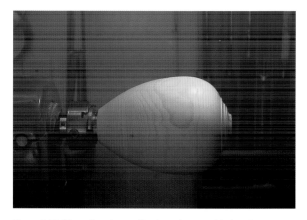

Figure 260. Note that the profile does change with the piece becoming "thinner."

Figure 258. Lowell started his vase from an ash log.

Getting Ready to Transfer the Measurement

Lowell's vase came to me sanded and with a light finish on it. (See Figure 261.) I roughed up the surface where the veneer inlay would go with some sandpaper. (See Figure 261.) I wanted the surface to take a pencil mark without difficulty.

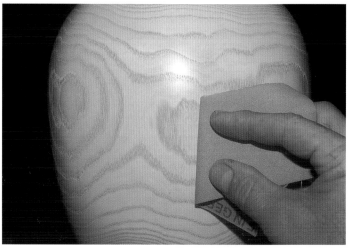

Figure 261. Lowell's vase came to me sanded and with a light finish on it. I roughed up the surface where the veneer inlay would go with some sandpaper so that the surface would take a pencil mark.

Figure 259. The vase was turned green with the pith in the middle.

Guide Lines and Transferring

Place some guidelines around the vase to help you position where the inlay should be placed. (See Figure 262.) Choose the prettiest place that will frame the inlay. Prepare a test veneer to use for drawing the curve. Use a sharp knife to score the back of the veneer (the unpapered side) about 1/16 of an inch. Use a straight edge to make straight cuts. Do not cut all the way through the veneer. Now spray water onto the test veneer. (See Figure 263.) The water combined with the relief cuts will make the veneer flexible enough so that it will curve in all directions.

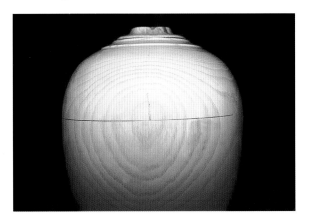

Figure 262. Draw some guidelines around the vase to help you position the inlay.

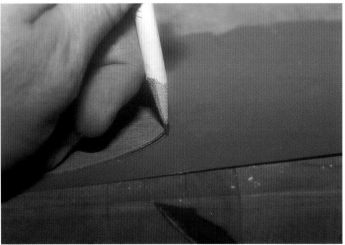

Figure 265. Trace the inlay pattern onto a piece of construction paper to make a good transfer pattern. .

Figure 263. Now spray water onto the test veneer to help it curve in both directions.

Place the veneer onto the vase, and use a very sharp pencil to scribe around the inlay. (See Figure 264.) To me, a better way to transfer the pattern is to scribe the shape onto a piece of construction paper. (See Figure 265.) Then cut out the pattern using a sharp pair of scissors.

Check your pencil pattern. Make sure that it is level and in the best possible position. (See Figure 266.) If you are not satisfied with the position, erase it and start over.

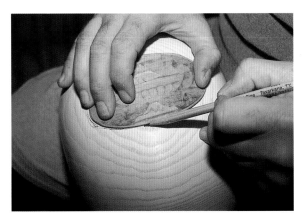

Figure 264. Place the veneer onto the vase, and use a very sharp pencil to scribe around the inlay.

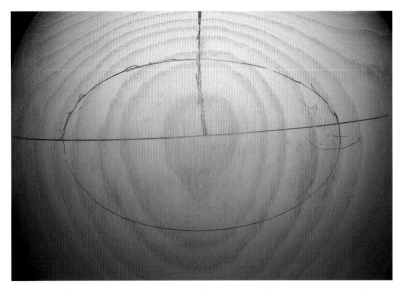

Figure 266. Check the transfer to make sure that it looks good and is positioned well.

The Knife Cut

The inlay rebate needs to be cut using a very sharp knife. This cut is critical; you may need magnification to see well. (See Figure 267.) Get into a very comfortable and stable position. Hold the vase firmly, and brace both hands against each other and the vase. (See Figure 268.) Make a straight in cut that is perpendicular to the surface of the vase. The cut should barely touch the inside of the pencil line. Carefully and slowly make this cut all the way around. The cut should be about 3/16 of an inch deep. **Do not slip while making this cut!** A slip cut into the vase will show, and blood on the vase will be hard to remove.

Figure 269. The rebate needs to be a uniform depth and needs to be cut smoothly. A miniature router is an ideal tool for this procedure.

Figure 267. The inlay rebate needs to be cut with a very sharp knife. This cut is critical; you may need magnification to see well.

Figure 270. Set the router bit height using your veneer as a guide. This will produce a very shallow rebate, which is all that you want.

Safety

Routers can be very dangerous. Do not let the router get away from you! It could quickly do severe damage to any body part that it came into contact with. Use a good face shield and respirator. (See Figure 271.) I like this combination shield and respirator. Ear protection is necessary when working with all noisy equipment. Use a good set of earmuffs. (See Figure 272.)

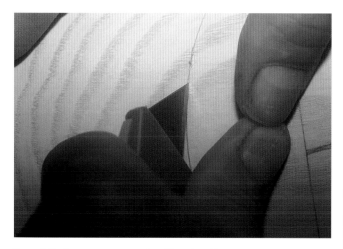

Figure 268. Get into a very comfortable and stable position. Hold the vase firmly, and brace both hands against each other and the vase.

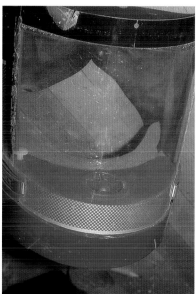

Figure 271. Routers can be very dangerous. Do not let the router get away from you! It could quickly do severe damage to any body part that it came into contact with. Use a good face shield and respirator.

Setting the Rebate Depth

The rebate needs to be a uniform depth and needs to be cut smoothly. A miniature router is an ideal tool for this procedure. I use a Sears mini-router designed for trimming laminates like Formica™. Use a 1/4-inch diameter straight cutting router bit. Be sure to tighten the router bit firmly, using the two wrenches provided. (See Figure 269.)

Set the router bit height using your veneer as a guide. (See Figure 270.) This will produce a very shallow rebate, which is all that you want.

Figure 272. Ear protection is necessary when working with all noisy equipment. Use a good set of earmuffs.

Test Cut

Make a test cut on a piece of scrap wood to check the depth of the router bit. (See Figure 273.) Here I drew the pattern shape on a piece of pine 2x4. I routed out the pattern and then inserted the inlay to check for depth. This check was perfect. Next, make a very small cut in the center of the vase. (See Figure 274.) Since you are cutting a round vase, the roundness of the vase will seat up inside the base of your router. This will cause the router to cut deeper than it does when cutting on a flat surface. Adjust the height of the router bit accordingly.

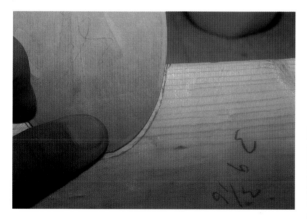

Figure 273. Do a test cut on a piece of scrap wood to check the depth of the router bit. Here I drew the pattern shape on a piece of pine 2x4. Route out the pattern, and then insert the inlay to check for depth.

Figure 274. Route out the rebate, starting from the center of the pattern.

Routing the Rebate

Hold the router firmly in both hands. Use both forearms to securely hold the vase. Make router cuts from the center of the pattern outward. Make small counterclockwise circles with the router. Use very good lighting and magnification to make sure that you can see well. You should be able to route very closely to the pencil line/cut mark. In most cases the wood chipped out where I had made the knife cut. Do not let the router get away from you and cross the pencil/knife cut.

Now even out any unevenness in the floor of the rebate. I like to use a flat sanding pad with 60-grit sandpaper to even out the floor of the rebate. Use sharp chisels to square up the floor of the rebate bed. (See Figure 275.) Use a sharp flat-end chisel to square up any irregularity in the wall of the rebate. (See Figure 276.)

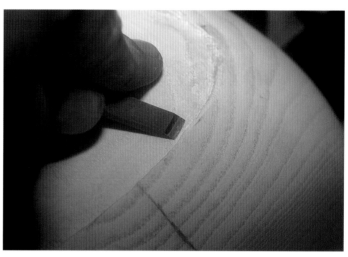

Figure 275. Use sharp chisels to square up the floor of the rebate bed.

Figure 276. Use a sharp, flatend chisel to square up any irregularity in the wall of the rebate.

61

Test Fitting the Inlay

Test fitting the inlay can be difficult since you do not want to moisten the inlay or the wood. Use a piece of construction paper to cut an exact pattern of the inlay. Place the inlay into the rebate to check for fit. Remember that the inlay curves in three dimensions. (See Figure 277.) Make light pencil marks and arrows to show where the rebate is too small. (See Figure 277.) Use your router to very carefully remove the excess wood.

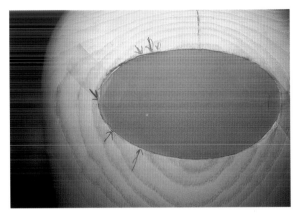

Figure 277. Use a construction paper pattern to check for fit. Make light pencil marks and arrows to show where the rebate is too small.

Gluing the Veneer Inlay

I used contact cement for this project. (See Figure 278.) Apply a layer of contact cement to the veneer inlay. (See Figure 279 – notice the thin relief knife cuts that go across the inlay.) Apply a layer of contact cement to the rebate. (See Figure 280.) Allow the cement to become tacky. Be sure to follow the instructions of the manufacturer.

Figure 278. Use a good quality contact cement or hide glue to glue the inlay.

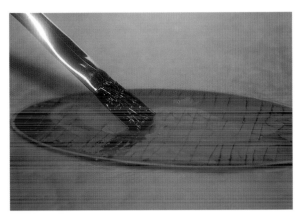

Figure 279. Apply a layer of contact cement to the veneer inlay.

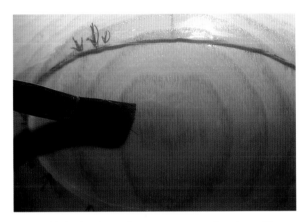

Figure 280. Apply a layer of contact cement to the rebate. Allow the cement to become tacky. Be sure to follow the instructions of the manufacturer.

Carefully place the inlay into the center of the rebate. Press it in using firm thumb pressure. Work the inlay into the rebate evenly from the center outward. (See Figure 281.) The contact cement will allow you some freedom of movement if you need to make minor adjustment in placement. Once the inlay is correctly placed, you might want to tack the veneer in place using cyanoacrylic glue and an accelerator. (See Figure 282.) Allow the glue to firmly set.

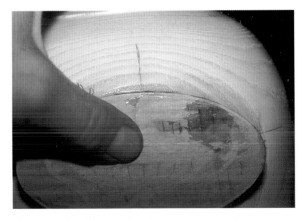

Figure 281. Carefully place the inlay into the center of the rebate. Press it in using firm thumb pressure. Work the inlay into the rebate evenly from the center outward.

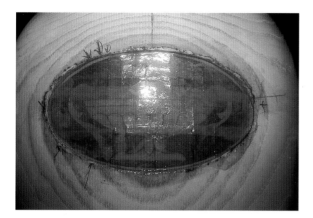

Figure 282. The contact cement will allow you some freedom of movement if you need to make a minor adjustment in placement. Once the inlay is correctly placed, you might want to tack the veneer in place using cyanoacrylic glue and accelerator. Allow the glue to firmly set.

Final Sanding

Use a flat sanding pad or sander to sand the edges around the inlay flat. (See Figure 283.) The Dremel™ sander with the flat sanding head on it is very good for this procedure. Be careful not to sand into the veneer since it is so thin. Work your way around the inlay, sanding all edges smooth and flat. (See Figure 284.) Then carefully sand through the paper backing that is covering the front of the inlay. Sand to 400-grit sandpaper.

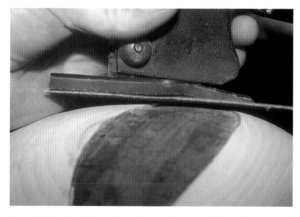

Figure 283. Use a flat sand pad or sander to sand the edges around the inlay flat.

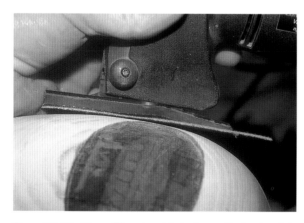

Figure 284. The Dremel™ sander with the flat sanding head on it is very good for sanding the edges flat. Carefully sand through the paper backing that is covering the front of the inlay. Sand to 400-grit sandpaper.

Finishing

Use the finish of your choice. I used Deft cellulose diluted 50/50 with lacquer thinner. I sprayed it on with an inexpensive spray gun to get a good finish. (See Figure 285.) Spray numerous light coats to get a good finish. I allow the coat to dry forty-five minutes before applying another light coat. Four to six coats produce a very nice finish. (See Figure 286.)

Figure 285. Use the finish of your choice. I used Deft cellulose finish diluted 50/50 with lacquer thinner and an inexpensive spray gun.

Figure 286. Spray numerous light coats to get a good finish. I allow the coat to dry forty-five minutes before applying another light coat. Four to six coats produce a very nice finish.

Conclusion

Congratulations, you have mastered a difficult turning and inlaying technique. This is a high skill level project. You should be proud of your progress. Your work will stand out from the crowd, and you will have the satisfaction of knowing that your artwork is beautiful and admired by many.

Gallery

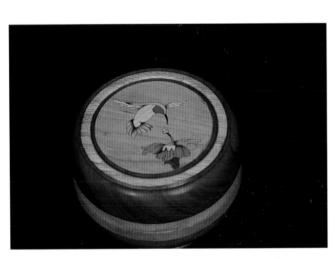

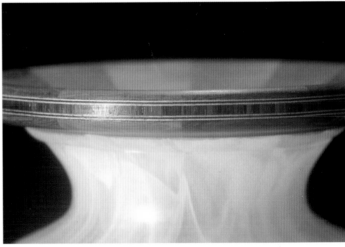